Homemaker's Menu of the Month Cookbook

HM homemaker's MENU of the MONTH COOKBOOK

edited by
Dana McCauley

KEY PORTER BOOKS

National Library of Canada Cataloguing in Publication

The Homemaker's menu of the month cookbook / edited and selected by
Dana McCauley ;
concept developed by Dianne Rinehart.

Includes index.
ISBN 1-55263-463-9

1. Cookery. 2. Menus. I. McCauley, Dana II. Rinehart, Dianne

TX728.H65   2002   642'.1   C2002-904190-2

THE CANADA COUNCIL | LE CONSEIL DES ARTS
FOR THE ARTS | DU CANADA
SINCE 1957 | DEPUIS 1957

ONTARIO ARTS COUNCIL
CONSEIL DES ARTS DE L'ONTARIO

*The publisher gratefully acknowledges the support of the Canada Council for the Arts
and the Ontario Arts Council for its publishing program.*

*We acknowledge the financial support of the Government of Canada through the
Book Publishing Industry Development Program (BPIDP) for our publishing activities.*

Key Porter Books Limited
70 The Esplanade
Toronto, Ontario
Canada M5E 1R2

www.keyporter.com

Design: Counterpunch
Printed and bound in Canada

02   03   04   05   06   5   4   3   2   1

Preface

When *Homemaker's Magazine* was launched 36 years ago, it aspired to provide readers with the best recipes from Canada's most famous food editors and writers. Among those who have edited our food section are the famous Jehane Benoît, Julie Aitken, Cynthia Wine, Carol Ferguson and, of course, our current food editor, Dana McCauley, co-author of the best-selling *Last Dinner on the Titanic* and author of *Pantry Raid*, who compiled the recipes for this book.

The result of their efforts and those of contributing food writers such as Rose Murray, Bonnie Stern and Barb Holland has been to delight millions of readers across the country with each new issue. In fact, some of our readers have built dinner clubs around the Menus of the Month you see featured in these pages.

Margaret Hamlett of Alexandria, Ontario, for example, meets with a group of eight friends every month to "share good company and good eating," each of them making a different course from the Menu of the Month. "I have to tell you it has been an overwhelming success, allowing us to attempt recipes that otherwise might have been read with interest, filed in 'interesting recipes to try' but then forgotten," she wrote.

And then there's Judy Fountain of Uxbridge, Ontario, who told us how *Homemaker's* recipe for Brussels Sprout Leaves in Whisky-orange Sauce allowed her to win a challenge posed by one of her dinner-club members to find a brussels sprout recipe that was actually "edible."

I know you'll enjoy the menus Dana has compiled and will refer to them to delight your guests time and time again. So dig in!

– Dianne Rinehart, Editor-in-Chief,
Homemaker's

Introduction

It is with great pride and excitement that I write this introduction to the *Homemaker's Menu of the Month Cookbook*. The task of choosing menus for this project was both daunting and enjoyable, since I was faced with a plethora of excellent material to choose from. Each time I looked over a past issue of the magazine, I got lost in it, savouring the many delicious recipes that have been published by the food editors and food writers whose creativity and commitment to excellence and accuracy have made *Homemaker's Magazine* the Canadian institution it is today.

For over 35 years, *Homemaker's Magazine* has been bringing reliable, of-the-moment recipes to Canadians. During that time, the perspectives and needs of home cooks have changed a lot. Events since the turn of the century have brought about a renewed spirit of sharing and community that makes entertaining at home as important today as it was in 1966, when we began publishing recipes. That said, while hospitality and sharing a good meal with family and friends are still virtues Canadians hold dear, today's hosts are looking for very different qualities in the menus they choose to serve. Lengthy preparations and elaborately contrived dishes have given way to simpler recipes formulated for more eclectic palates. On the one hand, our society has become more casual; few people today devote much concern to invitations, seating arrangements or other entertaining formalities when planning small dinner parties. On the other hand, culinary tastes and the general level of wine appreciation among ordinary Canadians are much more sophisticated than they were a generation ago. As a result, some of the classically inspired dinners our food writers conjured up 35 years ago seem quaintly old fashioned by today's well-travelled *Homemaker's* readers.

Homemaker's Menu of the Month Cookbook is a collection of 24 of our favourite recently published menus; this selection aims to offer readers a balance between casual, fun menus and more elegant entertaining fare. These special meals are divided into seasonal categories so that it's easy to find fresh, wonderful foods that will speak to the hearts and palates of your guests no matter when you decide to entertain. Each menu is accompanied by wine-matching guidelines written by the food and wine matchmaking experts at the Liquor Control Board of Ontario. These tools will ensure that it will be easy to match the perfect beverage to the meal you choose to prepare. So get ready to invite some friends in for supper; if you follow these menus in order, you're bound to have your most delicious (and possibly your most social!) year ever.

Cheers!

– Dana McCauley, Food Editor,
Homemaker's

Contents

SPRING

After a long winter by the fire, it's wonderful to welcome spring by hosting a dinner party. Although Easter and Passover offer two ideal opportunities to gather with friends and family and reconnect over a plate of good food, just celebrating the longer days is a great reason to entertain in springtime, too.

In this vast country of diverse climates, spring arrives at different times in different regions. While Vancouver tulips can be blooming in early April, it's just as likely that in other Canadian cities, snowstorms will still be snarling rush-hour traffic until late in the month and that it will take the warmer days of May to turn lawns green. Such unpredictable weather inspires many Canadians to take vacations to exotic locations each spring. For those of us who can't wait out the end of winter in the South Pacific, we can make the best of it by pausing to enjoy a good meal with friends.

So to accommodate both impulses – the celebration of spring and our impatience to get on with it already – this chapter highlights not only the pleasures of fresh, delicious springtime ingredients such as asparagus and lamb but also offers menus that can be used to create culinary adventures that provide brief escapes to warmer lands. Both types of occasion call for lighter fare on the table than the comfort foods served during winter and an easier, fresher approach to dressing the dining table.

Table accents and small touches can create a springtime feel even before dinner is served. If I could, I'd mow Holland to the ground and have spring flowers such as tulips, crocuses and daffodils in every nook to help create a fresh, fun, colourful ambience for springtime gatherings. That said, I caution you to avoid bouquets of overtly fragrant blooms such as hyacinths and paper whites, which will overwhelm the smell of delicious foods cooking. Other easy touches that can make your salute to spring successful include choosing light-coloured napkins and tableware or simply switching from heavy tablecloths to fabric or bamboo placemats.

St. Patrick's Day Pub Dinner

Whether you're celebrating St. Patrick's Day or just looking for a way to take the chill out of the Ides of March, welcome the gang by creating a cosy but lively at-home pub setting. Go all out and create a traditional pub atmosphere with dartboards and Celtic music, or just enjoy the evening relaxing together around the Blarney Stone.

MENU

Seafood Bar: Steamed Mussels, Oysters on
the Half Shell, Smoked-salmon Spread

Deep-dish Pub Pies

Pickled Beets and Pickled Onions
(purchased)

Irish Cream Caramel

Seafood Bar

Fresh oysters and mussels, as traditionally served in the seaside pubs and café-bars of Britain and Europe, make very popular appetizers for a casual party. Set out the seafood as a help-yourself buffet along with baskets of sliced crusty baguette and dark bread. Provide hot sauce and lemon wedges to accompany the oysters and mussels, small forks for the mussels, a large bowl for empty shells and lots of small napkins.

Steamed Mussels

4 lb (2 kg)	mussels
1/2 cup (125 mL)	each water and white wine
1	small onion, peeled and chopped
2	cloves garlic, minced
1/4 cup (50 mL)	chopped fresh parsley

Scrub mussels well; remove beards. Discard any mussels that are not tightly closed. Combine water, white wine, onion and garlic in a large pot. Bring to a boil. Add mussels, cover and steam, shaking pot occasionally, until shells open, 4 to 5 minutes. Discard any that don't open. Sprinkle mussels with parsley. Transfer mussels to large bowl or platter using a slotted spoon. Makes 8 appetizer servings.

Smoked-salmon Spread

In some markets, you can buy end chunks of smoked salmon,
which are much less expensive than the sliced version and fine
for this recipe. Smoked trout can also be used.

8oz (250 g)	cream cheese
1/4 cup (50 mL)	light sour cream
2 tbsp (30 mL)	lemon juice
2 tsp (10 mL)	horseradish
8 oz (250 g)	smoked salmon
3 tbsp (45 mL)	chopped fresh dill (approx)
3 tbsp (45 mL)	chopped fresh chives or green onions
3 tbsp (45 mL)	capers, chopped
	Salt and pepper

Blend cream cheese, sour cream, lemon juice and horseradish until
smooth in a food processor or with an electric mixer. Cut salmon into
chunks and add to bowl. Blend until almost smooth. Stir in dill, chives
and capers. Add salt and pepper to taste. Transfer to bowl, cover and
refrigerate for up to 2 days. To serve, garnish with fresh dill. Makes about
2 cups (500 mL).

Oysters on the Half Shell

Recruit someone adept with an oyster knife to shuck the oysters just before serving. When shucking, retain liquid in bottom shell; discard top shell. Slide knife
under each oyster to sever it from the shell. Serve on bed of ice. Accompany with
lemon wedges and hot pepper sauce.

Deep-dish Pub Pies

Take stodgy meat pies to exciting new heights with these individual make-ahead casseroles of beer-braised beef crowned with puff pastry.

2 lb (1 kg)	boneless blade, cross-rib or round steak, cubed
1/2 cup (125 mL)	all-purpose flour
2 tsp (10 mL)	salt
1 tsp (5 mL)	pepper
3 tbsp (45 mL)	vegetable oil (approx)
1 cup (250 mL)	chopped onions
2	cloves garlic, minced
3 cups (750 mL)	beef broth
1	bottle or can beer (about 12 oz/340 mL), preferably ale
1 cup (250 mL)	plain tomato sauce
1 tbsp (15 mL)	Worcestershire sauce
1	bay leaf
1/2 tsp (2 mL)	thyme
2	carrots, diced
3	potatoes, diced
3/4 cup (175 mL)	diced celery
1 1/2 cups (375 mL)	halved small mushrooms

Topping:

1	package frozen puff pastry (about 14 oz/400 g), thawed
1	egg, lightly beaten

Combine flour, salt and pepper in a plastic bag. Add beef and shake to coat with flour. Reserve remaining flour. Heat 1 tbsp (15 mL) of the oil in a large, heavy saucepan set over medium heat. Brown beef cubes in batches, adding more oil as needed. Add onions and garlic and cook until softened. Add broth, beer, tomato sauce, Worcestershire sauce, bay leaf and thyme. Bring to a boil, stirring well to scrape brown bits from bottom of pan. Reduce heat, cover and simmer for about 1 hour or until meat is nearly tender. Add carrots, potatoes and celery, cover and simmer for 30 minutes, then add mushrooms and simmer for 15 minutes longer or until meat and vegetables are tender.

Mix reserved flour mixture with a little cold water until smooth. Stir into beef mixture and bring to a boil, stirring. Simmer for about 5 minutes. Remove bay leaf. Taste and adjust seasoning. Divide beef mixture between 8 individual casseroles (each about 10 oz/300 mL or 4 inches/10 cm in diameter). Cover with foil. (Beef mixture may be refrigerated, before or after filling casseroles, for up to 2 days.)

Topping:
Preheat oven to 400F (200C). Roll out puff pastry to 1/8-inch (3 mm) thickness and cut into 8 rounds that are the same diameter as the casserole dishes (pastries will puff up during baking and shrink slightly in diameter). Place on large baking sheet. Chill until pastry is cold, about 15 minutes. Brush with lightly beaten egg. Bake in preheated oven for about 12 minutes or until puffed and golden brown; reserve. (Pastries may be made up to a day ahead. Cover with a tea towel and store at room temperature.)

Bake foil-topped casseroles in 400F (200C) oven for 15 minutes or until bubbling hot. Remove foil, top each with reserved puff pastry rounds and return to oven for 5 minutes. Serve hot. Makes 8 pies.

Irish Cream Caramel

Irish Cream liqueur adds a spirited touch to classic crème caramel. If you prefer to leave out the liqueur, replace it with an equal quantity of whipping cream and add 2 tsp (10 mL) of vanilla. This is a lovely cool-and-creamy dessert to serve with coffee after the hearty pub fare.

Caramel:

1 1/3 cups (325 mL)	granulated sugar
1/3 cup (75 mL)	water

Custard:

1 2/3 cups (400 mL)	2% milk
2/3 cup (150 mL)	35% whipping cream
2/3 cup (150 mL)	Irish Cream or similar liqueur
5	eggs
3	egg yolks
1/3 cup (75 mL)	granulated sugar
Pinch	salt

Caramel:

Preheat oven to 350F (180C). Combine sugar and water in a heavy saucepan or skillet. Heat over medium-high heat, stirring often, until sugar has dissolved. Continue to cook, without stirring, until mixture turns dark golden brown. Remove from heat and immediately pour equal portions of the syrup into eight 6-oz (175 mL) ramekins or custard cups, swirling to coat bottom of each with caramel (it will harden quickly). For easy cleanup of saucepan, add hot water and bring to a boil to dissolve caramel residue.

Custard:

Combine milk, cream and Irish Cream in a large glass measuring cup or microwaveable bowl. Heat in microwave oven or in a saucepan on the stove until hot but not boiling (if a skin forms, strain through sieve).

Whisk eggs, egg yolks, sugar and salt in a large bowl until just combined. Slowly add hot-milk mixture, stirring with whisk (for a smooth texture, don't whisk until frothy). Pour into caramel-lined cups.

Place cups in a large baking pan. Pour boiling water into pan to come halfway up sides of cups. Bake in 350F (180C) oven for 20 to 25 minutes or until knife inserted in custard comes out clean. Remove cups from water, let cool, then refrigerate until cold, about 3 hours. To unmould, run knife around edge of each custard and invert onto serving plate; caramel will run down sides of custard. Makes 8 servings.

What to Serve With St. Patrick's Day Pub Dinner

Guinness and oysters is one of these classic pairings that has stood the test of time and is a perfect match to our Seafood Bar. This rich stout also has enough character and structure to carry the Pub Pies, pickles and cabbage slaw.

If a lighter style beer is your preference, then choose a lager. Typically lighter-bodied, lagers' crisp acidity and elegant carbonation make them the perfect match the assortment of flavours and textures in the Seafood Bar, and they act as the perfect palate cleanser for the spices and pungent flavours in the condiments and side dishes.

To complement the dessert, try serving an ounce or two of Irish whisky in sweetened coffee; top with whipped cream – the perfect match to dessert.

Indonesian Escape

The central part of Bali is a tropical, lush paradise filled with heavily scented blooms. The food, like the landscape, is exotic and richly spiced – perfect for a dinner party for winter-weary friends who want to pretend that summer is already here. Create a lush outdoor atmosphere by decorating with potted plants, exotic blooms and batik or woven bamboo table accessories.

MENU

Balinese Fish Satays on Lemon Grass Stalks

Indonesian Glazed Pork Ribs

Yellow Rice

Mixed Vegetable Salad With
Spicy Toasted Coconut

Caramel-banana Cream Pie

Balinese Fish Satays on Lemon Grass Stalks

Unlike the strips of meat North Americans usually call satays, Balinese satays are made with seasoned ground meat or fish shaped around aromatic lemon grass or sugar cane skewers. This version features fish as well as the perfumy flavours of ginger and kaffir lime leaves.

17	lemon grass stalks
4	shallots or 1 small onion, chopped
3	cloves garlic, chopped
2 tbsp (30 mL)	vegetable oil
1 tsp (5 mL)	brown sugar
1 tsp (5 mL)	minced gingerroot
2 tbsp (30 mL)	lime juice
1/2 tsp (2 mL)	cinnamon
1/4 tsp (1 mL)	nutmeg
Pinch	cloves
1	fresh, frozen or dried kaffir lime leaf
3/4 tsp (4 mL)	each salt and pepper
1 cup (250 mL)	fresh bread crumbs
1 1/2 lb (750 g)	fresh cod or monkfish fillet
2	green onions, finely chopped
1	egg white, beaten

Peel one lemon grass stalk until you reach the tender inner stalk, and chop. Mince any tough parts near the top. Combine lemon grass with shallots, garlic, vegetable oil, brown sugar, gingerroot, lime juice, cinnamon, nutmeg, cloves and lime leaf (if using dried, rehydrate in 1 tbsp/15 mL boiling water) in a blender or food processor. Blend until almost smooth.

Transfer to a small saucepan and bring to a boil. Reduce heat to medium and simmer for 3 to 4 minutes, stirring often. Cool to room temperature. Stir in bread crumbs.

Chop the fish very finely using a sharp knife. Mix with green onions, egg and lemon grass mixture until well combined. Tightly cover and refrigerate for 1 hour or overnight.

Cut remaining lemon grass stalks into 6-inch (15 cm) lengths and peel, using a vegetable peeler, into a spear shape. Spoon about 2 tbsp (30 mL) of the fish mixture into your hand and shape into a ball. Press around a stalk of lemon grass so that it looks like an elongated football. (May be prepared to this point, covered and refrigerated for up to 12 hours.)

Preheat the broiler to high. Lightly grease a nonstick baking sheet and place satays on top. Cook, turning once, for 7 to 8 minutes or until browned. Makes about 2 dozen satays.

Kaffir lime leaves, lemon grass and exotic spices such as cardamom can be hard to find even in urban centres. Unfortunately, these unique tropical flavours are also hard to replace with substitutes.

If you have trouble finding such items, try visiting your city's Chinatown or a local Asian market. Kaffir lime leaves are sold frozen or dried in many Asian markets even if fresh are unavailable. Likewise, frozen, chopped lemon grass can now be found in many stores even if the fresh stalks are not available in the produce section.

Spices such as cardamom and turmeric are sold in many grocery and bulk stores. A bulk store is an ideal place to buy them if you use them infrequently, since you can purchase them in small amounts.

Indonesian Glazed Pork Ribs

These deliciously gooey ribs are reminiscent of Indonesian spit roasted suckling pig but much more manageable for home cooks.

6 lb (2.7 kg)	pork back ribs (about 4 racks)
2	bay leaves
1 tsp (5 mL)	peppercorns
1	onion, chopped
1 1/2 cups (375 mL)	ketchup
1/2 cup (125 mL)	hoisin sauce
3 tbsp (45 mL)	lemon juice
2 tbsp (30 mL)	each Worcestershire and soy sauce
1 tbsp (15 mL)	Dijon mustard
2 tsp (10 mL)	fish sauce
4	cloves garlic, minced
2 tsp (10 mL)	cumin
1 tsp (5 mL)	cayenne

Preheat oven to 350F (180C). Combine ribs, bay leaves, peppercorns and onion in a large roasting pan. Add enough cold water to cover. Cover tightly with foil and place in preheated oven. Cook for 1 hour or until ribs are tender enough to pierce easily with a fork. Cool in cooking liquid. Drain off liquid and transfer ribs to a platter.

Stir ketchup with hoisin sauce, lemon juice, Worcestershire sauce, soy sauce, mustard, fish sauce, garlic, cumin and cayenne in a bowl. Preheat grill to medium-high. Lightly grease.

Brush sauce evenly over ribs. (Ribs can be prepared ahead to this point, covered and refrigerated for up to 2 days.) Place on grill and cook, basting often and turning as needed, for about 10 minutes or until well glazed and heated through. Alternatively, bake in preheated 325F (160C) oven in a single layer for 25 to 30 minutes. Makes 6 servings.

Yellow Rice

This exotic rice dish is a crucial element in a Javanese rice festival. Traditionally served moulded into a cone shape, it is pretty and mildly spiced.

1	can coconut milk (14 oz/400 mL)
4 cups (1 L)	boiling water
3 cups (750 mL)	long-grain rice
2 tbsp (30 mL)	butter
1	onion, thinly sliced
1 tsp (5 mL)	turmeric
1 tsp (5 mL)	salt
Pinch to ¼ tsp (1 mL)	ground cardamom
Pinch	cloves
1	2-inch (5 cm) piece lemon grass, finely chopped

Whisk coconut milk into boiling water until all lumps are dissolved. Let cool and reserve. Wash and drain rice. Heat butter in a large saucepan set over medium heat. Add onion and cook for 5 minutes or until softened. Increase heat to medium-high and cook for 2 minutes more or until it starts to become golden. Stir in turmeric, salt, cardamom, cloves and lemon grass. Add rice and stir-fry for 1 minute.

Pour in reserved coconut mixture and bring to a boil. Stir and reduce heat to low. Cover and simmer for 15 minutes. Remove from heat and let stand, covered, for 5 minutes. Fluff with a fork. Makes 6 to 8 servings.

Mixed Vegetable Salad
With Spicy Toasted Coconut

While the crisp green lettuce salads we are familiar with in Canada are not commonly served in Bali, this type of dish, served warm or at room temperature, is very popular at multi-course meals.

¼ cup (50 mL)	shaved or slivered unsweetened coconut
¼ tsp (1 mL)	hot sauce
3 tbsp (45 mL)	vegetable oil
3	paper-thin slices gingerroot
1	large shallot, finely chopped
1 tsp (5 mL)	brown sugar
2	cloves garlic, thinly sliced
2 cups (500 mL)	snow peas, halved on the diagonal
2 cups (500 mL)	asparagus, cut into 1-inch (2.5 cm) lengths
2 cups (500 mL)	small button mushrooms or sliced mushrooms
2 cups (500 mL)	baby corn cobs, halved lengthwise
1	yellow pepper, thinly sliced
2 tbsp (30 mL)	soy sauce
	Lime wedges

Preheat oven to 300F (150C). Toss coconut with hot sauce. Spread on a baking tray. Roast for 3 to 5 minutes or until golden; reserve.

Heat oil in a wok or deep skillet set over medium heat. Add ginger, shallot, brown sugar and garlic. Cook for 3 minutes or until slightly softened. Increase heat to high. Add snow peas, asparagus, mushrooms, corn cobs and pepper slices. Stir-fry for 5 minutes or until pepper is beginning to brown. Add soy sauce and toss to coat. Turn into a serving dish. Sprinkle with coconut and serve with lime wedges on the side. Makes 6 servings.

Caramel-banana Cream Pie

Indonesian desserts are very different from the usual pies and cakes we serve in North America. Jellied coconut desserts and super-thickened butterscotch-flavoured custard concoctions are popular items. This decadent pie, inspired by established Balinese flavours and traditions, has a more familiar Western-style format.

Pastry:

1 1/2 cups (375 mL)	all-purpose flour
1/2 tsp (2 mL)	salt
1/2 cup (125 mL)	cold butter, cubed
1	egg
1 tsp (5 mL)	white vinegar
	Ice water

Filling:

1/2 cup (125 mL)	all-purpose flour
1/3 cup (75 mL)	granulated sugar
Pinch	salt
2 cups (500 mL)	hot milk
2	egg yolks
1 tbsp (15 mL)	butter
1 tsp (5 mL)	vanilla
1/2 cup (125 mL)	unsweetened whipped cream
1/4 cup (50 mL)	caramel-lime sauce (recipe follows)
2	small ripe bananas

Topping:

1 cup (250 mL)	whipped cream
	Banana slices
	Caramel-lime sauce

Pastry:

Combine flour and salt in a food processor fitted with metal blade. Using the pulse button, cut in butter until mixture resembles coarse crumbs. Beat egg with vinegar in a measuring cup; add enough ice water to measure 1/3 cup (75 mL). Add to flour mixture and process until dough begins to clump.

Turn dough onto a piece of plastic wrap and wrap tightly so that it forms a ball. Refrigerate until chilled through. Roll pastry between two pieces of waxed paper, flipping occasionally, into a 10-inch (25 cm) wide circle. Line a 9-inch (23 cm) pie plate with pastry, turning edges under to make a rim. Chill for 15 minutes.

Preheat oven to 400F (200C). Prick raw pie shell all over with a fork and line with foil and pie weights. Bake in preheated oven for 20 minutes, remove foil and weights and bake for 10 minutes longer or until golden. Cool on a rack.

Filling:

Combine flour with sugar and salt in a saucepan. Whisk in milk until smooth and place pan over medium heat. Stirring constantly, cook until thick, about 5 to 8 minutes. Remove from heat.

Pour a little of the milk mixture into the egg yolks and whisk until well combined and smooth. Pour into milk mixture and set over low heat. Stirring constantly, cook from 3 to 5 minutes or until very thick and just bubbling. Remove from heat. Stir in butter and vanilla. Cover with plastic wrap touching surface. Cool completely. Fold whipped cream into custard and reserve.

To assemble: Scrape caramel-lime sauce (recipe follows) into cooled pie shell; spread evenly. Slice bananas thinly and place in the bottom of the prepared shell. Spread cream filling over top. Chill until set.

Decorate pie with whipped cream and thin banana slices. Drizzle with additional caramel-lime sauce if you like. Makes 8 servings.

Caramel-lime Sauce:

Lime peel cuts the richness of this sumptuous sauce.

1/2 cup (125 mL)	granulated sugar
2 tbsp (30 mL)	water
1/4 cup (50 mL)	warm whipping cream
1 tsp (5 mL)	vanilla
1/2 tsp (2 mL)	finely grated lime peel

Combine sugar and water in a small saucepan. Set over medium-high heat. Stir gently until sugar is dissolved. Bring to a boil without stirring. Boil for 7 to 10 minutes or until syrup turns a deep amber. Immediately remove from heat. Shield hand with an oven mitt or tea towel and whisk in warm cream. Stir in vanilla. Cool completely. Stir in lime peel. Makes 1/2 cup (125 mL).

What to Serve With Indonesian Escape

Beer is traditionally the preferred thirst-quencher to drink with these spicy Asian dishes, and we recommend European-style wheat beers. Many brewers also make this style of beer right here in Canada.

With the Balinese Fish Satays on Lemon Grass Stalks, serve a wheat ale. This crisp and slightly creamy lighter ale has enough lemony lift to complement the lemon grass component while accenting the mild, spicy, sweet character of this dish. Or if you're not a beer fan, try a dry Riesling, with its fresh, citrusy flavour and ever-so-slight sweetness.

For the Pork Ribs, Yellow Rice and Mixed Vegetable Salad, a Belgian-style wheat beer, which offers a fuller-bodied, slightly spicier style – enough to stand up to the rich flavours – that is ideal. Alternatively, try a spicy and intensely aromatic off-dry wine such as a Gewürztraminer.

Australian Adventure

No meal is more typically Aussie than a barbecue. A casual gathering around the barbie – whether on a picnic, a camping trip, a beach, a backyard deck or an apartment balcony – celebrates much that Australians hold dear: the great outdoors, a wonderful climate, good company, fabulous food and excellent wines and beers.

Canadian cooking today could be described in much the same way. So why not precede the arrival of summer with an Aussie-style barbecue that feels right at home in Canada, even if our spring weather dictates that the party be indoors?

MENU

Grilled Prawns and Chicken Satays With
Spicy Dipping Sauce

Grilled Swordfish Steaks and Lamb Chops

Grilled Vegetable Platter

Crunchy Cucumber Salad

Fresh Fruit Salad With
Coconut Custard Cream

Grilled Prawns and Chicken Satays
With Spicy Dipping Sauce

Large shrimp (called prawns in Australia) are perennial favourites for the barbie, and Asian foods such as satays are modern favourites in both Australia and Canada.

Dipping Sauce:

1/2 cup (125 mL)	each soy sauce, rice vinegar, brown sugar, peanut butter and coconut milk
2 tbsp (30 mL)	each minced garlic and gingerroot
	Asian chili sauce or hot pepper sauce to taste

Skewers:

1/4 cup (50 mL)	each rice vinegar and light-coloured soy sauce such as Kikkoman
2 tbsp (30 mL)	each brown sugar and vegetable oil
2	cloves garlic, minced
1 lb (500 g)	very large shrimp (12 to 24), peeled and deveined, tails left on
1 lb (500 g)	boneless, skinless chicken breasts, cut into strips about 1 inch (2.5 cm) wide
24	bamboo skewers (about 6 inches/15 cm long)

Dipping Sauce:

Combine soy sauce with vinegar, sugar, peanut butter, coconut milk, garlic, ginger and chili sauce in a blender until smooth. (Can be refrigerated up to a day; bring to room temperature before serving.)

Skewers:

Whisk vinegar with soy sauce, brown sugar, vegetable oil and garlic. Place shrimp and chicken separately in large zip-top plastic bags and refrigerate if not using immediately. Two to three hours before grilling, add half the marinade to the chicken. Turn to coat and let marinate in refrigerator.

Soak bamboo skewers in water for 30 minutes before grilling. About 10 minutes before grilling, add the remaining marinade to the shrimp and turn to coat. Remove chicken strips from marinade and thread onto 12 skewers. Remove shrimp from marinade and thread onto remaining skewers.

Grill over medium-high heat, turning occasionally, until just cooked through (about 5 minutes for chicken, 3 to 4 minutes for shrimp). Serve with dipping sauce. Makes about 24 skewers.

Grilled Vegetable Platter

Choose a colourful mixture of vegetables such as sweet red and yellow peppers, green and yellow zucchini, small eggplants and red onions. Cut into thick slices, brush lightly on all sides with olive oil, and sprinkle lightly with salt and pepper. Grill, turning once, for 3 to 6 minutes or until lightly browned and tender-crisp. Remove to a large platter. Drizzle with a little olive oil and balsamic or red-wine vinegar. Sprinkle lightly with salt, pepper, a little minced garlic, if desired, and chopped fresh herbs such as oregano, rosemary and thyme. (Can be prepared up to an hour ahead and served at room temperature.)

The mixed grill (traditionally sausages, steaks and lamb chops) is a long-time favourite at Aussie barbecues. Our menu updates this classic with meaty fish steaks alongside lamb chops. The herbed marinade can be used for both the fish and the lamb, and the recipe makes enough for guests to have some of each.

1/2 cup (125 mL)	each white wine, lemon juice and olive oil
4	cloves garlic, minced
1/4 cup (50 mL)	each chopped fresh mint and oregano
1 tsp (5 mL)	pepper
6	swordfish or other fish steaks (about 1 inch /2.5 cm thick and about 6 oz/175 g each)
12	loin lamb chops, about 1 inch (2.5 cm) thick
	Salt and pepper to taste

Whisk white wine with lemon juice, olive oil, garlic, mint, oregano and pepper. (Marinade can be covered and refrigerated for up to 8 hours.) Place fish steaks and lamb chops separately in large, heavy zip-top plastic bags or in shallow dishes large enough to hold them in a single layer (refrigerate if not using immediately). About 2 hours before grilling, pour half the marinade over lamb chops and turn to coat. Marinate in refrigerator until 30 minutes before grilling. About 10 minutes before grilling, pour remaining marinade over fish steaks and turn to coat.

Remove fish steaks and lamb chops from marinade. Place on greased grill over medium-high heat. Grill for 4 to 5 minutes on each side or until fish is just cooked through and lamb is medium-rare (for medium or well-done, cook a few minutes longer). Makes 6 small servings of fish and lamb.

Crunchy Cucumber Salad

Upstage traditional salads such as coleslaw with this fresh-tasting combination. It can be varied by adding other crunchy vegetables – shredded cabbage, strips of Belgian endive or the crisp inside leaves of romaine lettuce, for example. Small, firm "Lebanese cucumbers" are popular in Australia; a long, seedless cucumber will substitute well here.

4 oz (125 g)	sugar snap peas or small snow peas
1	unpeeled seedless cucumber
3	stalks celery, sliced
1	small fennel bulb, sliced into strips
3	green onions, sliced

Dressing:

1/3 cup (75 mL)	olive oil
3 tbsp (45 mL)	fresh lemon juice
1	clove garlic, minced
2 tsp (10 mL)	each chopped fresh tarragon and basil (or 1/2 tsp/2 mL dried)
	Salt and pepper to taste

Blanch peas in boiling water for 1 to 2 minutes or just until tender-crisp. Drain and refresh under cold water; drain well. Quarter cucumber lengthwise and cut into 1/4-inch (5 mm) slices. Combine peas, cucumber, celery, fennel and onions in a large bowl. Cover tightly with plastic wrap and refrigerate.

Dressing:

Whisk olive oil with lemon juice, garlic, tarragon and basil; cover and refrigerate. Up to 1 hour before serving, toss salad with dressing. Add salt and pepper to taste if needed. Refrigerate. Makes 6 to 8 servings.

Fresh Fruit Salad With Coconut Custard Cream

Choose a gorgeous mixture of tropical and other fruits in season (mango, papaya, figs, starfruit, pineapple, peaches, apricots, kiwi, strawberries, raspberries). Cut the fruit into bite-size chunks. Drizzle with a little lime juice and sweeten to taste. Stir in some passion fruit pulp if available. Spoon into a large serving bowl, individual dessert glasses or coconut shells.

For a touch of tradition (Aussies still love their traditional puddings and custards), accompany the fruit salad with a bowl of custard sauce for topping. For an updated version that is delicious with fruit, make this tropical version:

Coconut Custard Cream: Prepare a soft custard (from scratch or from custard powder), substituting canned coconut milk for half the milk in the recipe. Stir in some freshly grated coconut (fresh has the best flavour and texture, but packaged will do) and a few drops of almond or coconut extract. Pour into a bowl, cover and chill (custard will thicken; if too thick, whisk in a little more milk). If desired, serve with a garnish of shaved fresh coconut on top.

What to Serve With Australian Adventure

This menu from "sunshiny" down under calls for rich-tasting wines with tropical fruit flavours. For the Grilled Prawns and Chicken Satays, for instance, serve a wine with some oak influence, such as an Australian Marsanne that offers inviting tropical fruit flavours, a hint of apple and a "food friendly" structure wrapped in vanilla-rich oak.

The Swordfish Steaks are well matched with either a red or white wine. White-wine choices would include a full-bodied Australian Chardonnay with buttery apple and pear aromas, a nice oak balance and a mellow finish. Alternatively, try an oaked Semillon that has lots of ripe tropical fruit, a rich creamy texture and a deliciously long finish. Red-wine fans can serve Merlot, which has a nice red berry fruit, soft tannin and a clean finish. With the lamb, red is an optimum choice. Cabernet Sauvignon offers rich cassis and dark berry tones on the nose, soft vanilla and ripe fruit on the palate and a well-balanced, spicy finish.

Get into the spirit of this Aussie escape menu by using down-under terms for the foods you serve. The blokes (guys) and sheilas (girls) you invite will enjoy it! This glossary gives you some of the basic words that apply to this menu.

Prawns:	large shrimp
The barbie:	barbecue
Courgettes:	zucchini
Aubergine:	eggplant
Cos lettuce:	romaine lettuce
Capsicums:	yellow and red peppers

Spring Fling

Who said eating healthfully and stylish
entertaining couldn't be combined?
This lively, fresh-flavoured menu features
plenty of colourful foods as well as
many of the important nutrients
everyone needs to tune up both body
and soul and to feel good for spring.

MENU

Spring Tonic Soup

Rosemary-orange Roasted Spring Chicken

Braised Asparagus, Leeks and New Potatoes

Spring Salad With Flowers

April Fool

Spring Tonic Soup

This easy-to-make soup includes the traditional spring-tonic ingredients – chicken broth, eggs, lemon and vitamin-rich greens to prime you up for working in the garden and taking bike rides through the park.

2	cans (10 oz/284 mL each) chicken broth (low-fat, low-sodium, diluted with water) or 5 cups (1.25 L) chicken broth
2	eggs
2 tbsp (30 mL)	fresh lemon juice
2 cups (500 mL)	coarsely chopped fresh greens
	Salt and pepper

Bring chicken broth to full boil in a stainless steel or enamel pot. Whisk eggs with lemon juice in a bowl. Remove boiling broth from heat. Whisk 1/4 cup (50 mL) broth into egg mixture, then slowly pour mixture back into pot, whisking constantly. Stir in greens and season with salt and pepper to taste, if needed. Serve immediately or keep warm over very low heat so that it does not curdle. To serve chilled, let cool to room temperature, then refrigerate until very cold. Makes 6 servings.

Tip: When making Spring Tonic Soup, try fresh sorrel (if available) for the greens; it has a wonderfully fresh lemony taste. A combination of young spinach or chard with watercress or arugula is also very good.

Rosemary-orange Roasted Spring Chicken

After roasting on a bed of vegetables, orange slices and
rosemary, this chicken is incredibly moist and tender. It's also
very impressive to present at the table when garnished with
additional orange slices and fresh herbs.

1	roasting chicken (5 to 6 lb/2.5 kg)
1	unpeeled orange, cut into wedges
1	onion, cut into wedges
	Fresh rosemary (two 6-inch/15 cm branches)
	Salt and pepper
1	each carrot and celery stalk, coarsely chopped
1	onion, sliced
1	unpeeled orange, sliced
1 ½ cups (375 mL)	chicken broth
2 tbsp (30 mL)	cornstarch (optional)

Preheat oven to 450F (230C). Trim any excess fat from chicken. Squeeze
juice from orange wedges into cavity of chicken, then place the squeezed
wedges in the cavity alternately with onion wedges and half the rosemary,
ending with an orange wedge to close the opening. Sprinkle skin with salt
and pepper. Place carrot, celery, onion slices, orange slices and remaining
rosemary in the centre of a lightly greased roasting pan. Set chicken on top.

Place in preheated oven and immediately reduce heat to 375F (190C).
Roast for 1 3/4 to 2 hours or until an instant-read thermometer registers
180F (82C) when inside of thigh is pierced. Remove chicken to a platter
and cover with foil.

Add chicken broth to mixture remaining in roasting pan. Place pan over
medium-high heat. Heat, stirring, until simmering. Press pulp from
orange slices into the sauce; remove orange peels and rosemary. Carve
chicken into portions and serve sauce on the side. Makes 6 servings.

Braised Asparagus, Leeks and New Potatoes

You don't have to live close to the woods to enjoy the delectable wild leeks (also called ramps) recommended for this recipe, since many urban markets now sell them as a specialty item each spring.

1	large bunch fresh asparagus (about 30 stalks)
3	medium (or 12 wild) leeks
18	tiny new red potatoes, halved
1 tbsp (15 mL)	each butter and olive oil
3/4 cup (175 mL)	chicken broth
	Salt and pepper

Wash asparagus well and trim off tough ends; reserve. Trim dark green tops from leeks, leaving white and light green parts only. Trim away roots, leaving enough of root end intact that leeks don't fall apart when quartered. Cut into quarters lengthwise (if using wild leeks, leave whole). Wash thoroughly.

Boil potatoes in a pot of boiling, salted water for 5 minutes or until almost tender. With a slotted spoon, remove potatoes to a plate. In the same water, boil asparagus for 2 minutes; add asparagus to potatoes.

Melt butter with oil in a large skillet set over medium heat. Add leeks and cook, stirring often, for 3 minutes. Add potatoes, asparagus and broth, increase heat and bring to a boil. Boil over medium-high heat, shaking pan often, for about 4 minutes or until vegetables are tender and liquid has disappeared. Add salt and pepper to taste. Makes 6 servings.

Spring Salad With Flowers

Fresh flowers add beautiful colour and a desirable bitter or peppery flavour to a salad. Packages of edible flowers are available at many greengrocers, or you can pick blossoms from houseplants such as pansies and violets as long as they have not been sprayed with pesticides.

3 tbsp (45 mL)	balsamic vinegar
1 tbsp (15 mL)	lemon juice or white-wine vinegar
1 tbsp (15 mL)	pure maple syrup
1 tsp (5 mL)	Dijon mustard
1/2 tsp (2 mL)	salt
	Pepper to taste
3/4 cup (175 mL)	olive oil
6 cups (1.5 L)	mesclun or mixed salad greens such as young spinach, bibb lettuce, mâche, frisée and arugula
	Edible flowers in assorted colours (about 18)

Whisk together balsamic vinegar, lemon juice, maple syrup, mustard, salt and pepper. Slowly whisk in oil until well blended.

Combine greens and flowers in a large salad bowl. Just before serving, toss with enough dressing to coat the leaves. Makes 6 servings.

April Fool

Traditional fools are made with whipped cream swirled with puréed, sweetened fruit. This low-fat version uses thickened yogurt and only a splash of cream, so it is definitely a wise person's choice.

2 cups (500 mL)	low-fat yogurt
2 tbsp (30 mL)	granulated sugar (approx)
1/2 cup (125 mL)	whipping cream
3/4 cup (175 mL)	raspberry purée (recipe follows) or maple syrup
	Toasted almonds or crushed maple sugar candy
	Edible flowers

Place a large sieve over a bowl and line sieve with a paper coffee filter or double layer of cheesecloth. Place yogurt in sieve, cover with plastic wrap and let drain, refrigerated, for 6 to 8 hours or until thickened and reduced to about 1 cup (250 mL). Discard liquid. Place thickened yogurt in large bowl and stir in sugar, adding more to taste if desired.

Whip cream until stiff peaks form and fold into yogurt. Fold in raspberry purée or maple syrup very gently with spatula to create a marbled effect; be careful not to blend too much. Transfer mixture to a serving bowl and chill for at least 1 hour. If desired, just before serving, sprinkle surface with almonds or maple sugar candy and garnish with a few flowers. Makes 6 servings.

Raspberry Purée:

Thaw a 10-oz (300 g) package of frozen, unsweetened raspberries. Press through sieve to remove seeds. Stir in 2 tbsp (30 mL) granulated sugar.

What to Serve With Spring Fling

Sparkling wine is the perfect start to our Spring Fling. A good Canadian Brut sparkler typically offers a combination of clean citrus flavours balanced by crisp acidity and a lively sparkle that is the perfect start to any meal. It serves not only as a great aperitif but also as an excellent accompaniment to the Spring Tonic Soup.

The Rosemary-orange Roasted Spring Chicken has appealing rosemary/ green herb elements and orange and roast vegetable flavours that will harmonize well with a New-World Sauvignon Blanc. This style of wine offers a wonderful combination of citrus, melon, tropical fruit and herb-tinged flavours that are a terrific match to this dish, its accompaniments and, if you must, the salad.

If red is your preference, try a light bodied Chianti. Here the forward, fresh berry flavours and earthy notes allow this wine to harmonize with the majority of dishes in this menu, while its acidity and structure cleanse the palate.

The April Fool recipe gives the option of using either raspberry or maple syrup. Our matching is a pair of domestic products that vary according to your selection of ingredient. If you choose raspberries, then a great match is Southbrook's Framboise. Its lusciously sweet raspberry flavours meld perfectly to the flavours and richness in the dessert. If instead you select maple syrup, then try Oh Canada Maple Liqueur, which easily matches the sweetness and plays off the flavours in the dessert.

Stocking a Spring Pantry

With spring comes a shift in appetites that necessitates a shift in our shopping habits. Use this checklist to remind yourself of the pleasures of spring you may want to include on your next shopping list:

- asparagus
- extra-virgin olive oil
- fiddleheads
- early-spring herbs such as tarragon,
    parsley and chives
- greens such as watercress, sorrel and
    lamb's lettuce
- lamb, veal and fish
- lemons
- morels and other wild mushrooms
- new potatoes
- white-wine vinegar
- wild leeks (also called ramps)

Easy and Elegant
for Easter

Seasonal celebrations and the warmer weather make
springtime ideal for getting together with family and
friends for a celebratory meal. This modern collection
of Easter recipes is colourful and fresh-tasting but
also satisfying enough to hold its own if the
weather is chilly.

MENU

Chiffonade Salad on Belgian Endive Points

Sunflower-encrusted Lamb

Roasted Asparagus and Tomatoes

Individual Scalloped Potato Gratins

Ruby-red Grapefruit Tart

As pretty as a spring flower, this salad makes a lovely opener for a spring dinner party.

Dressing:

4 tsp (20 mL)	cider vinegar
1	small clove garlic, minced
1/4 tsp (1 mL)	each salt and pepper
1/3 cup (75 mL)	extra-virgin olive oil

Salad:

1 head	radicchio
3 cups (750 mL)	shredded arugula or spinach leaves
1	lemon
1/2 cup (125 mL)	crumbled blue cheese
2	Belgian endives (about 6 oz/175 g)

Dressing:

Whisk vinegar with garlic, salt and pepper. Drizzle in olive oil, whisking constantly; reserve.

Salad:

Separate radicchio into leaves and cut out sturdy white vein. Stack leaves and shred finely with a sharp knife. Combine with arugula. Using a zester, remove long strips of peel from lemon. Add to salad. Toss with cheese to combine.

Cut stem ends from Belgian endives. Separate into individual leaves, reserving tiny hearts for another use. Wash and pat endive points dry. Arrange in a circle, points out, on a large platter. Drizzle dressing over salad and toss gently. Arrange in centre of platter. Serve immediately. Makes 6 servings.

Sunflower-encrusted Lamb

The relationship between seeds and springtime is well established. In this recipe, that symbolism also tastes great, as the sunflower seeds add a delicious crunch and a nutty flavour to a classic spring roast.

3 lb (1.5 kg)	rack of lamb, Frenched
3/4 tsp (4 mL)	each salt and pepper
1/4 cup (50 mL)	Dijon mustard
2 tbsp (30 mL)	each chopped fresh mint and rosemary
2 tsp (10 mL)	olive oil
3	cloves garlic, minced
1/2 cup (125 mL)	unsalted sunflower seeds

Preheat oven to 425F (220C). Pat lamb dry if moist. Sprinkle salt and pepper all over lamb. Combine mustard with mint, rosemary, olive oil and garlic. Rub mixture all over the fleshy side of lamb. Press sunflower seeds into mustard mixture. Place lamb, bone side down, on a rack set over a rimmed baking sheet. Place in the centre of preheated oven.

Roast for about 25 minutes or until internal temperature registers 140F (60C) on an instant-read thermometer. Let rest for 5 minutes. Place rack on a cutting board and use a heavy knife to slice between bones to separate into chops. Makes 6 servings.

Tip: Lamb racks are sometimes sold with the fat cap on. The fat cap is a thick, gristly layer surrounded by fat that covers the fleshy side of a rack. It is impossible to eat. If lamb racks come with the fat cap on, slice it away with a sharp knife and discard before seasoning the rack with salt and pepper.

Roasted Asparagus and Tomatoes

Tiny grape, or currant, tomatoes are now available in most grocery stores. They are wonderfully sweet on their own, but roasting intensifies their flavour, which complements the balsamic vinegar and thyme used to season this easily made side dish.

2 tbsp (30 mL)	each olive oil and balsamic vinegar
1 tsp (5 mL)	dried thyme leaves
1	clove garlic, minced
1/2 tsp (2 mL)	each salt and pepper
1/4 tsp (1 mL)	brown sugar
2 cups (500 mL)	grape or cherry tomatoes
2	bunches asparagus

Preheat oven to 300F (150C). Whisk olive oil with balsamic vinegar, thyme, garlic, salt, pepper and sugar. Cut tomatoes in half and toss to combine with olive-oil mixture. Spread tomatoes in a roasting pan and place in preheated oven. Cook, stirring occasionally, for 30 minutes or until tomatoes are shrivelled.

Break the ends from the asparagus stalks at the natural breaking point. Add tender lengths of asparagus to tomatoes and continue to cook for 25 minutes or until asparagus is tender. (Can be prepared to this point, covered and refrigerated for up to 2 days. Reheat just before serving or serve at room temperature.) Makes 6 servings.

Individual Scalloped Potato Gratins

Golden, bubbly scalloped potatoes made in individual dishes look as wonderful on dinner plates as they do in the cooking dish.

3	strips bacon
2 tsp (10 mL)	vegetable oil
1	large onion, peeled and finely chopped
2	green onions, finely chopped
1 1/4 cups (300 mL)	35% whipping cream
1/2 tsp (2 mL)	each salt and pepper
6	potatoes, peeled and very thinly sliced (about 1 1/2 lb/750 g)
1/2 cup (125 mL)	shredded Gruyère cheese

Preheat oven to 350F (180C). Finely chop bacon and heat oil in a skillet set over medium-high heat. Add bacon and cook, stirring often, for 5 minutes or until crisp. Reduce heat to medium and add onion. Cook, stirring often, for 5 minutes. Stir in green onions; reserve.

Stir cream with salt and pepper. Grease 6 ramekins or 12 large muffin tins. Layer potatoes alternately with bacon mixture so that you have 3 layers of potato and 2 layers of bacon mixture in each container. Press down firmly. Pour an equal amount of cream mixture into each cup.

Place ramekins on a rimmed baking sheet. Cover tightly with foil and bake for 35 minutes. Remove cover and sprinkle cheese evenly over top of potatoes. Bake for 20 to 30 minutes longer or until potatoes are fork-tender. Makes 6 servings.

Ruby-red Grapefruit Tart

Bracing yet sweetly satisfying, the filling for this tart is a gorgeous deep pink colour that no one will be able to resist.

Crust:

1 cup (250 mL)	all-purpose flour
3 tbsp (45 mL)	granulated sugar
1/2 cup (125 mL)	cold butter, cubed
1	egg, beaten

Filling:

8	egg yolks
1 cup (250 mL)	granulated sugar
1/4 cup (50 mL)	cornstarch
1/2 cup (125 mL)	grenadine
2 cups (500 mL)	fresh red grapefruit juice
1 tbsp (15 mL)	finely grated grapefruit peel
2 tbsp (30 mL)	butter

Crust:

Combine flour and sugar. Cut in butter until mixture resembles coarse crumbs. Stir in egg. Press mixture together with hands until a smooth dough forms. Roll to fit a 10-inch (25 cm) flan pan with removable

bottom or a 9-inch (23 cm) pie plate. Prick pastry all over with a fork. Chill for 20 minutes.

Preheat oven to 375F (190C). Bake on lower rack of preheated oven for 12 to 15 minutes or until lightly golden.

Filling:

Whisk egg yolks until smooth and reserve. Blend sugar, cornstarch, grenadine, grapefruit juice and peel in a saucepan until well combined. Place over medium-high heat and cook, stirring gently, until thickened, about 5 to 10 minutes.

Whisk in eggs and cook, stirring constantly, for 2 minutes. Stir in butter. Cool to room temperature. Scrape into prepared pie shell. Makes 8 servings.

What to Serve With Easy and Elegant for Easter

Wine is often a difficult match for salad because of the vinegar component in most dressings. However, the Chiffonade Salad on Belgian Endive Points employs a cider vinegar along with crumbled blue cheese, making it very "wine friendly." A white wine such as an off-dry Vidal will marry well with the stimulating salty-bitter components of this starter dish.

Sunflower-encrusted Lamb demands a full-bodied Spanish red. Try a robust Tempranillo such as a Spanish Rioja or Ribero del Duero. An alternative, which would also pair very nicely with the Roasted Asparagus and Tomatoes, is a Cabernet Franc, with balanced herbaceous, peppery flavours.

White-wine fans should try a Pinot Gris from Alsace. Rich and intense, these wines have enough body to stand up to the flavour of the lamb and will complement the Scalloped Potato Gratins.

The zesty Ruby-red Grapefruit Tart requires a wine with clean citrus flavours, lively acidity, some sweetness and substantial body. Ontario Late Harvest Rieslings with luscious grapefruit/apricot/citrus flavours, lively acidity and well-balanced sweetness are the perfect foil for this finale.

Fireworks Buffet

The Victoria Day weekend is a celebratory time for summer-hungry Canadians. To commemorate the first long weekend of the summery season, this party menu has been designed for broad appeal. Suited to serve casually outdoors, it's ideal for an evening spent watching the fireworks with family and friends. Although each dish turns out picture-perfect, there are many shortcuts and make-ahead tips so that *you* can enjoy the party as much as your guests.

MENU

Stuffed Tomato, Endive and Cucumber Canapés

Tropical Curry Dip

Green Rocket Salad

Firecracker Noodle Salad

Grilled "Roman Candle" Kabobs

Ice-cream-cone Butterscotch Sundaes

Stuffed Tomato, Endive and Cucumber Canapés

This recipe offers a stylish presentation of a classic Greek salad.

4 oz (125 g)	feta cheese
¼ cup (50 mL)	chopped, pitted black olives
3 tbsp (45 mL)	best-quality extra-virgin olive oil
2 tbsp (30 mL)	finely chopped fresh oregano or 2 tsp (10 mL) dried oregano leaves
1 tsp (5 mL)	finely grated lemon peel
1	clove garlic, minced
¾ tsp (4 mL)	coarsely ground black pepper
1	seedless cucumber
6	small Roma or very small vine-ripened yellow or red tomatoes
1	head Belgian endive

Crumble feta into a medium-sized bowl. Gently stir in olives, olive oil, oregano, lemon peel, garlic, pepper and salt. (Can be combined to this point, covered and refrigerated for up to 1 day.)

Slice cucumber into 1/2-inch (1 cm) thick pieces. Using a spoon, scoop out enough of the centre of each slice to make a bowl shape.

Halve tomatoes and gently squeeze out seeds. Cut base from Belgian endive and separate leaves. Rinse under cold water and pat dry.

(Vegetables can be prepared, covered and refrigerated up to 4 hours ahead.)

Spoon cheese mixture into cucumbers, tomatoes and endive before serving. Makes about 4 dozen canapés.

Tropical Curry Dip

As unusual as it sounds, this dip is very easy to like. Serve it with raw veggies, apple wedges or crackers.

2 tsp (10 mL)	butter
3	green onions, chopped
1	large ripe banana, peeled and chopped
2 tsp (10 mL)	mild Indian curry paste
1 tsp (5 mL)	brown sugar
1/4 cup (50 mL)	pressed coconut
1 tbsp (15 mL)	lime juice
1 cup (250 mL)	sour cream
1/2 tsp (2 mL)	salt
	Pepper

Melt butter in a small saucepan set over medium heat. Add the onions and cook, stirring often, for 2 minutes.

Stir in banana, curry paste and brown sugar. Cook, stirring, for about 1 minute or until well combined.

Transfer banana mixture to the bowl of a food processor or blender. Crumble in pressed coconut and add lime juice. Process until smooth.

Add sour cream and salt and mix until combined. Season with pepper to taste. Can be made ahead, covered and refrigerated for up to 1 day. Makes 2 cups (500 mL).

Green Rocket Salad

Riotously colourful, this salad of peppery lettuces and sweet yellow peppers literally explodes with flavour.

2	bunches arugula or 4 cups (1 L) torn Boston lettuce
1	small head radicchio
1/2 cup (125 mL)	thinly sliced red onion
1	yellow or orange pepper, thinly sliced

Dressing:

2 tbsp (30 mL)	balsamic vinegar
1 tsp (5 mL)	finely chopped fresh rosemary
1/4 tsp (1 mL)	each salt and pepper
1/4 cup (50 mL)	extra-virgin olive oil

Wash arugula in cold water until all the grit is removed. Spin or pat dry. Remove long stems and place leaves in a large serving bowl. Tear radicchio into bite-size pieces.

Add radicchio, onion and pepper to arugula. Toss until well combined. (Can be prepared to this point, covered with a damp cloth and plastic wrap and refrigerated for up to a day.)

Dressing:

Whisk vinegar with rosemary, salt and pepper in a small bowl. Whisking, drizzle in olive oil until well combined.

Drizzle dressing over arugula mixture. Toss to coat evenly.
Makes 8 servings.

Firecracker Noodle Salad

This substantial noodle salad is pleasantly spicy and can stand in as a main course for vegetarians. If you prefer a milder taste, reduce the sambal olek and ginger by half and substitute a green pepper for the Cubanelle.

12 oz (375 g)	fresh chow mein noodles or 6 cups (1.5 L) cooked spaghetti
1/4 cup (50 mL)	vegetable or chicken broth
1/4 cup (50 mL)	sesame oil
2 tbsp (30 mL)	medium sherry
2 tbsp (30 mL)	finely grated gingerroot
1 tbsp (15 mL)	sambal olek or chili-garlic sauce
1 tbsp (15 mL)	each light soy sauce and lime juice
1 tsp (5 mL)	granulated sugar
1	each Cubanelle, red bell and banana peppers
1/2	red onion, quartered and thinly sliced

Boil noodles for 2 minutes or until al dente. Drain well and fluff with a fork. Meanwhile, stir broth with sesame oil, sherry, gingerroot, sambal olek, soy sauce, lime juice and sugar in a large bowl.

Add peppers, onion and noodles. Toss to combine. Makes 8 servings.

Grilled "Roman Candle" Kabobs

Kabobs are ideal for outdoor dining, since they can be eaten with a knife and fork or standing up if the meal is buffet-style.

4 lb (2 kg)	skinless, boneless chicken breasts
1	each red and green peppers
2	bunches green onions
3/4 cup (175 mL)	buttermilk or yogurt
2 tbsp (30 mL)	Dijon mustard
1 tbsp (15 mL)	freshly grated lemon peel
1 tbsp (15 mL)	vegetable oil
1	clove garlic, minced
1 tbsp (15 mL)	chopped fresh thyme
1 tsp (5 mL)	ground black pepper

Soak about 2 dozen long wooden skewers in water for 15 minutes. Cut chicken into 1-inch (2.5 cm) chunks. Quarter peppers and discard seeds, stem and white core. Cut into large chunks. Slice green ends from onions and reserve for another use. Chop root from ends of onions and cut remaining white and light green part into 1-inch (2.5 cm) lengths.

Thread equal amounts of each ingredient onto skewers, alternating meat with vegetables. Place in a shallow baking dish.

Stir buttermilk with mustard, lemon peel, vegetable oil, garlic, thyme and black pepper. Pour over kabobs. Turn skewers to coat each one evenly. Place in refrigerator for at least 2 hours or up to 2 days.

Preheat grill to medium-high. Lightly grease, using a paper towel saturated with vegetable oil. Place kabobs on grill. Cover and cook, turning often, for 12 to 18 minutes or until chicken is cooked through. Makes 8 servings.

Ice-cream-cone Butterscotch Sundaes

This dessert-buffet idea will please kids of all ages.

8	waffle-style cones
4 cups (1 L)	premium vanilla ice cream
1/2 cup (125 mL)	butterscotch sauce
1/2 cup (125 mL)	whipped cream
8	maraschino cherries
1/2 cup (125 mL)	each chopped toasted pecans, crushed chocolate bars, shredded coconut, candy sprinkles (optional)

Scoop ice cream into cones and drizzle with butterscotch sauce. Top each cone with a dollop of whipped cream and a cherry. Let guests decorate their sundaes with toppings of their choice. Makes 8 servings.

What to Serve With Fireworks Buffet

For a pre-dinner burst of flavour, serve Campari or Dubonnet over ice with a splash of soda water and a twist of lemon, lime or orange peel. Versatile Riesling is a perfect match for the Stuffed Tomato, Endive and Cucumber Canapés, the Tropical Curry Dip, and the Green Rocket Salad.

For red-wine lovers, try a lightly chilled Gamay/Zwiegelt blend to complement the Grilled "Roman Candle" Kabobs. This unoaked, berry-filled, peppery wine is a perfect match for sweetly piquant grilled peppers and is mild enough for the grilled chicken. If white is your preference, try a Semillon with herbal, floral and peach flavours that are full, rich and complex.

End this meal with a wee bit of Frangelico liqueur in coffee as you await the fireworks.

SUMMER

The miracle of the Canadian summer is that it can be as intensely warm and sultry as winter is blustery and cruel. I suspect I'm like many Canadians: during the coldest winter spells, I pine for warm evenings when you can serve a fresh, luscious meal on the patio or terrace and then linger over the table nibbling and talking with family and friends into the wee hours. In the summer, it's better than wonderful to relax outside with a satisfied stomach, breathing in the honeysuckle.

Every region of Canada has its own summer specialties: juicy Okanagan cherries, succulent Saskatoon berries, sweet Ontario tomatoes, intense Quebec blueberries and meaty Newfoundland lobsters are just a handful of the excellent ingredients available in this country in the summer. The wealth of wonderful local produce grown in all parts of Canada means that cooks can unbridle their creativity during this season of extra-long evenings.

While grilling is an increasingly popular way for Canadians to prepare food during the summer, this chapter features a diverse range of summer menus that highlight grilled foods as well as lean poached dishes and salads galore. From a casual Saskatchewan family picnic to an upscale summer-celebration menu, there is something here for every summer occasion, whether it be a self-catered wedding or an impromptu cookout. The menus in this chapter also include inspirations from vineyards and spice chests, so truly there is something here for everyone!

Whether you're cooking for family or friends during the summer, remember to keep everything fresh and simple. Even formal parties can be easygoing at this time of year. Choose exciting table accessories with vibrant colour palettes, modern aluminum and stainless steel accent pieces such as trays and baskets, and gauzy, diaphanous, cool fabrics in crisp bright and natural whites to make your summer dinner parties sizzle with style!

Co-op Cookout

"You bring a salad, I'll do dessert" has become a standard plan for relaxed summer get-togethers of family and friends. A potluck barbecue – with the hosts taking care of the main course and everyone else contributing a side dish – is easy and enjoyable for all. Here's a co-operative menu of do-ahead, portable dishes filled with summery flavours to match up with grilled steaks (or your favourite grilled chicken, pork or lamb).

MENU

Grilled Quesadillas

Grilled Steaks

Mexicali Rice and Black-bean Salad

Zucchini-tomato Salad

Garlic Bread With Parmesan and Sun-dried Tomatoes

Strawberry-chocolate Mascarpone Trifle

Grilled Quesadillas

Assemble these tasty nibblers early in the day and spread them out on waxed paper, cover tightly and refrigerate until needed. Cut them into wedges and serve warm from the grill.

1	small red onion
1	large sweet red pepper
1/2	bulb fennel
1 tbsp (15 mL)	olive oil
1/2 tsp (2 mL)	each salt and black pepper
1/4 cup (50 mL)	chopped kalamata olives
1 tbsp (15 mL)	balsamic vinegar
2 tbsp (30 mL)	chopped fresh basil
6	flour tortillas (8 inches/20 cm)
6 oz (175 g)	soft goat cheese or light cream cheese
	Olive oil for brushing

Preheat oven to 425F (220C). Cut onion, pepper and fennel into 1/4-inch (5 mm) dice. Spread on rimmed baking sheet. Drizzle with oil and season with salt and pepper. Roast in preheated oven for 20 minutes, stirring occasionally, until vegetables are tender-crisp. Transfer to bowl. Stir in olives and vinegar. Cover and refrigerate. (Can be made to this point up to 3 days ahead.) Stir in basil.

Spread each tortilla with about 2 tbsp (30 mL) of the goat cheese. Sprinkle one half of each tortilla with about 1/4 cup (50 mL) of the vegetable mixture; fold tortillas in half, pressing down lightly. (Can be wrapped in plastic and refrigerated for up to 4 hours.) Brush quesadillas lightly with oil. Place on grill over medium heat (or cook in batches in large nonstick skillet) for 1 to 2 minutes per side or until toasted. Cut each into 6 wedges and serve warm. Makes 36 appetizers.

Mexicali Rice and Black-bean Salad

This colourful salad will please the whole crowd. Not only does it complement the rest of this summer menu, but it can also stand as a main course for any vegetarians who come to your cookout.

1 1/2 cups (375 mL)	basmati rice
3 cups (750 mL)	water
1 tsp (5 mL)	salt
1	can (19 oz/540 mL) black beans, rinsed and drained
2 cups (500 mL)	cooked corn kernels
1	each sweet red and green peppers, diced
3	jalapeño peppers, seeded and minced
1	red onion, diced
1 cup (250 mL)	light sour cream
1/4 cup (50 mL)	olive oil
1/4 cup (50 mL)	fresh lime juice
2 tsp (10 mL)	each dried oregano and ground cumin
2	avocados
1 cup (250 mL)	chopped fresh coriander leaves or parsley

Rinse rice in several changes of cold water; drain. Bring water to a boil in a medium saucepan. Add rice and salt. Reduce heat, cover and simmer for 15 minutes or until tender. Spread hot rice on baking sheet; let cool. Combine rice, black beans, corn, sweet peppers, jalapeños and onion in a large serving bowl.

Whisk sour cream with olive oil, lime juice, oregano and cumin. Pour over rice mixture and toss to coat well. Cover and refrigerate for up to 12 hours. Just before serving, peel and chop avocados. Add to salad along with coriander. Taste and add salt if needed. Makes 12 servings.

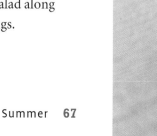

Zucchini-tomato Salad

This attractive salad is flavoured with a grainy mustard dressing and uses some of summer's most succulent produce. When making ahead, keep the dressing, tomatoes and zucchini separate and toss them together just before serving so that the salad won't become soggy.

6	medium zucchini (about 2 lb/1 kg)
4	green onions, chopped
8	plum tomatoes (about 1 1/2 lb/750 g)
1/2 cup (125 mL)	olive oil
1/4 cup (50 mL)	red-wine vinegar
2 tbsp (30 mL)	grainy mustard
2	cloves garlic, minced
2 tsp (10 mL)	granulated sugar
1/2 tsp (2 mL)	each salt and pepper
1/2 cup (125 mL)	chopped fresh parsley

Cut zucchini in half lengthwise and slice. Place in a bowl with the green onions. Cut tomatoes in half lengthwise and squeeze out the seeds. Cut into thin lengthwise strips and place in a separate bowl.

Whisk together oil, vinegar, mustard, garlic, sugar, salt and pepper. Stir in parsley. Just before serving, toss tomatoes with 1/4 cup (50 mL) of the dressing. Toss zucchini with remaining dressing and arrange in the centre of a serving platter or shallow serving bowl. Arrange tomato strips around the edge. Makes 12 servings.

Garlic Bread With Parmesan and Sun-dried Tomatoes

Sun-dried tomatoes and Parmesan cheese jazz up garlic bread and make it special for a gathering. Dress the loaves ahead so that they're ready to grill when you are.

1/3 cup (75 mL)	butter, softened
1/4 cup (50 mL)	freshly grated Parmesan cheese
1/4 cup (50 mL)	finely chopped sun-dried tomatoes
2 tbsp (30 mL)	finely chopped fresh parsley
2	cloves garlic, minced
1	large loaf French bread (about 18 inches/45 cm long and 4 inches/10 cm wide)

Blend together butter, Parmesan, tomatoes, parsley and garlic; reserve. Cut bread into 3/4-inch (2 cm) slices. Spread butter mixture on one side of each slice. Reassemble slices into loaf shape; wrap tightly in foil.

Place on grill over medium heat (or in 350F/180C oven), turning occasionally, for about 20 minutes or until heated through. Makes 24 slices.

Strawberry-chocolate Mascarpone Trifle

Strawberries are truly one of the natural gifts of summer. This impressive-looking dessert is easy to make and just gets better in the refrigerator, which makes it perfect for making ahead and taking to a party.

1 cup (250 mL)	mascarpone cheese
2/3 cup (150 mL)	granulated sugar
2 tbsp (30 mL)	orange juice
1 tbsp (15 mL)	grated orange peel
1 1/2 cups (375 mL)	whipping cream
4 cups (1 L)	sliced fresh strawberries
1/3 cup (75 mL)	orange liqueur or orange juice
1	frozen pound cake (10 oz/300 g)
4 oz (125 g)	bittersweet or semi-sweet chocolate, grated
	Whole strawberries
	Mint sprigs

Beat mascarpone with sugar, orange juice and peel until creamy. Whip cream in separate bowl. Fold whipped cream into mascarpone mixture; reserve. Combine strawberries and liqueur.

Cut cake into 1/2 -inch (1 cm) cubes. Arrange half of cubes in the bottom of an 8-cup (2 L) glass serving bowl. Top with half the strawberries, including juice. Spread with half the mascarpone mixture, then sprinkle with half the grated chocolate. Repeat layers.

Cover and refrigerate for at least 4 hours or up to 12 hours. Before serving, garnish with whole strawberries and mint sprigs. Makes 12 servings.

The Grilled Quesadillas require a cool and refreshing palate cleanser. Like a Mexican lager such as Corona. Served with the requisite wedge of lime this crisp, light beer acts as the perfect palate refresher.

If you prefer wine, pick an off-dry Riesling with vibrant fruit and mineral notes.

Grilled steaks harmonize best with Australian Shiraz. Assertive and lush, with jammy, berry fruit, this wine style marries well with the smoky flavours of the steaks while offering enough body to match their weight and texture. It's no wonder that the "Aussies" have a reputation for barbecuing!

The Zucchini-tomato Salad and Garlic Bread with Parmesan and Sun-dried Tomatoes calls for a Mediterranean-style wine such as well-chilled rosé from Provence, France, or Lirac or Tavel. If a red is your preference, then choose a lighter styled red from Greece such as a Nemea served cool.

For the Strawberry-chocolate Mascarpone Trifle, a ruby port will reflect the berry and chocolate flavours in the dessert wonderfully and have enough body and sweetness to match its richness while an orange liqueur will deliver comparable sweetness and flavours.

Grilling Steaks

The best steaks for grilling are rib, rib-eye, strip loin, tenderloin, T-bone, wing and sirloin. Use this chart to be sure your steaks are juicy and perfectly cooked every time. Rub steaks with olive oil and season with plenty of coarsely ground pepper and salt just before they hit the grate. Grill, turning only once or twice with tongs – never a fork – over medium-high heat.

THICKNESS	MINUTES PER SIDE		
	Rare	Medium	Well-done
1/2 to 3/4 inch (1 to 2 cm)	3–5	5–7	7–9
1 inch (2.5 cm)	5–7	7–9	9–11

Wine-Country Cooking

Whether you've spent a day meandering from winery to winery in the Okanagan Valley or the Niagara region, or whether you've been roller-blading around town before creating these recipes, this menu will evoke the mood of Canada's premier wine regions.

MENU

Spinach-wrapped Goat Cheese With Cherry-mint Salsa

Grilled Pita Wedges With Garlic and Cumin

Grilled Pork Tenderloin With Spicy
Apricot-rosemary Marinade

Fork-mashed New Potatoes With Mustard and Basil

Grilled Zucchini and Summer Squash
(recipe not included)

Panna Cotta With Riesling Summer-berry Compote

Spinach-wrapped Goat Cheese
With Cherry-mint Salsa

This intriguing salad is bursting with colour and complex flavours. If cherry season is past, substitute grapes for an equally delicious and fresh-tasting opener.

Cherry-mint Salsa:

1 1/2 cups (375 mL)	fresh sweet cherries, halved and pitted
1	small yellow pepper, diced
1	clove garlic, minced
1 1/2 tsp (7 mL)	grated gingerroot
2 tbsp (30 mL)	olive oil
1 tbsp (15 mL)	each fresh lime juice and red-wine vinegar
1 tsp (5 mL)	grated lime peel
1/2 tsp (2 mL)	red pepper flakes
1/4 tsp (1 mL)	each salt and pepper
1/4 cup (50 mL)	chopped fresh mint

Spinach-wrapped Goat Cheese:

12	large spinach leaves
8 oz (250 g)	goat cheese, chilled
1/4 tsp (1 mL)	each salt and pepper
1 tbsp (15 mL)	olive oil
3 cups (750 mL)	shredded fresh spinach

Cherry-mint Salsa:

Combine cherries, yellow pepper, garlic, ginger, olive oil, lime juice, vinegar, lime peel, pepper flakes, salt and pepper. Let stand for 1 hour for flavours to blend. Just before serving, stir in mint.

Spinach-wrapped Goat Cheese:

Trim stems and thick centre ribs of spinach leaves using a paring knife. Place leaves in a colander and pour boiling water over to wilt. Chill in cold water. Spread leaves, rib side up, on paper towels to dry. Cut cheese into 12 pieces and shape each into a flattened log. Arrange on the wide bottom end of the leaves. Season with salt and pepper. Fold over sides of spinach to cover cheese and roll up to enclose. (Bagged spinach can be used in this recipe; use two medium leaves instead of large ones and overlap sides to wrap the cheese.)

Brush with olive oil and place on greased grill over medium heat for 30 to 60 seconds per side or until soft and warmed through. Arrange shredded spinach on serving plates and spoon salsa over it. Arrange cheese on top. Serve immediately along with Grilled Pita Wedges With Garlic and Cumin. Makes 6 servings.

Grilled Pita Wedges With Garlic and Cumin

These little crostinis are perfectly crisp and yummy for scooping up any stray goat cheese in the salad.

4 tsp (20 mL)	olive oil
1	clove garlic, minced
1/4 tsp (1 mL)	each ground cumin and pepper
3	Greek-style (pocketless) pita breads

Combine olive oil, garlic, cumin and pepper. Brush over pita breads. Grill over medium-high heat for 1 to 2 minutes per side or until lightly browned. Cut breads into 6 wedges each and serve alongside salad. Makes 6 servings.

Grilled Pork Tenderloin
With Spicy Apricot-rosemary Marinade

Asian flavours add a modern complexity to this entrée. For a wonderful aroma and a deep woodsy, smoky flavour, add rosemary stems to your coals or place them on top of the grill itself while the pork is cooking.

³/₄ cup (175 mL)	sliced fresh apricots or plums
¹/₄ cup (50 mL)	orange juice
3 tbsp (45 mL)	each balsamic vinegar and brown sugar
2 tbsp (30 mL)	each soy sauce and vegetable oil
1 tbsp (15 mL)	each Asian chili paste and Worcestershire sauce
1 tbsp (15 mL)	chopped fresh rosemary
2	cloves garlic, minced
3	small pork tenderloins (about 10 oz/300 g each)

Combine apricots with orange juice, vinegar and brown sugar in a saucepan. Bring to a boil. Reduce heat, cover and simmer for 10 minutes or until apricots are tender. Purée in a food processor until smooth. Transfer mixture to large bowl. Stir in soy sauce, oil, chili paste, Worcestershire sauce, rosemary and garlic. Add pork and turn to coat well. Cover and marinate for up to 1 hour at room temperature or up to 1 day in refrigerator.

Remove pork from marinade. Place on greased grill over medium heat. Cook, turning and basting often with sauce, for 14 to 16 minutes or until just a hint of pink remains on the inside. Transfer meat to a cutting board and cut into diagonal slices. Makes 6 servings.

Fork-mashed New Potatoes
With Mustard and Basil

Meant to be chunky, not smooth like traditional mashed potatoes, this side dish will have a pleasantly earthy taste when made with farm-fresh potatoes.

2 1/2 lb (1.25 kg)	small new potatoes
1/3 cup (75 mL)	chopped fresh basil
1/3 cup (75 mL)	sour cream or buttermilk (approx)
4 tsp (20 mL)	Dijon mustard
1/2 tsp (2 mL)	salt
1/4 tsp (1 mL)	pepper

Cook potatoes in boiling salted water in a large saucepan for 20 minutes or until tender. Drain; place in a shallow bowl. Cut into quarters (leave peel on or off, as desired). Add basil, sour cream, mustard, salt and pepper. Roughly mash with a fork or lightly with a potato masher (there should be some lumps remaining). Serve immediately. Makes 6 servings.

Panna Cotta With Riesling Summer-berry Compote

Meaning "cooked cream" in Italian, panna cotta is a light, silky, eggless custard that is served cold.

Panna Cotta:

1	envelope unflavoured gelatin
2 tbsp (30 mL)	cold water
1 cup (250 mL)	each sour cream, whipping cream and light cream
1/3 cup (75 mL)	granulated sugar
1	vanilla bean
	Lemon balm or mint sprigs

Compote:

2 cups (500 mL)	raspberries
3/4 cup (175 mL)	Riesling wine
1/4 cup (50 mL)	honey
1 cup (250 mL)	blueberries or blackberries

Lightly oil six 5-oz (150 mL) ramekins; reserve. Sprinkle gelatin over cold water in a small bowl; reserve.

Combine sour cream, whipping cream, light cream and sugar in a saucepan. Halve vanilla bean lengthwise and scrape out seeds. Add seeds to cream mixture (add vanilla bean halves, if desired, for additional flavour). Place saucepan over medium heat, stirring often, until very hot, but do not let boil. Stir in gelatin mixture until dissolved. Remove vanilla bean halves (if using).

Pour into ramekins. Chill for 4 hours or until set. To serve, run a sharp knife around edges and turn out onto serving plates. Spoon Riesling summer-berry compote (recipe follows) around panna cottas. Garnish with lemon balm.

Compote:

Purée 1/2 cup (125 mL) of the raspberries with the wine in a food processor. Transfer to a small saucepan and add honey. Place over medium-high heat and bring to a boil. Reduce heat and simmer for 2 minutes. Strain mixture through a fine sieve into a bowl. Let cool slightly, then refrigerate until cold.

Add remaining fruit. Toss gently and let stand for up to 20 minutes to macerate. Makes 6 servings.

What to Serve With Wine-Country Cooking

The textures and flavours of Spinach-wrapped Goat Cheese with Cherry-mint Salsa make it a good partner for a crisp dry white wine such as Pouilly-Fumé, whose soft fruit flavours and fresh-cut grass aroma marry well with the cheese and fruit. Or, if you prefer something a little softer and not as crisp, choose a Pinot Blanc.

The Grilled Pork Tenderloin with Spicy Apricot-rosemary Marinade is nicely complemented by a Gamay Noir. Gamays have a refreshing juicy berry element that makes them popular in the summer.

Panna Cotta With Riesling Summer-berry Compote is a luscious dessert that brings out the best in Ontario's Late Harvest and Select Late Harvest wines. These styles of wine offer fresh peach, apricot and tropical fruit flavours balanced with lively acidity and a clean finish, which adds a nice dimension to the seasonal berries.

Fire and Spice

Written for true aficionados of flavour, this salmon-
barbecue menu uses common spices and herbs such as
ginger, cumin and coriander throughout the recipes,
but the way in which they are used
changes their character: spicy,
sweet, nutty, fragrant or piquant
tones emerge, depending
on the cooking technique.
Mint and citrus and
tropical fruits add
fresh flavours and
lightness that balance
the deeper spice notes.
By the time you and your
guests have finished this
complex and satisfying meal,
your palates are sure to be pleased.

MENU

Goat-cheese Dip With Tomato, Mint and
Coriander

Grilled Salmon With Dill and Mustard Seeds

Spiced Potato and Green-bean Salad

Warm Mushroom and Spinach Salad
With Fennel and Tomatoes

Mango-coconut Cake With
Yogurt-lime Cream

Goat-cheese Dip With Tomato, Mint and Coriander

Fresh mint, coriander, ginger and lime give a perky flavour to this tomato-topped goat-cheese appetizer. Spread it on pita bread, cucumber slices and pepper strips.

2	medium tomatoes, seeded and finely diced
1/4 cup (50 mL)	thinly sliced green onions
2 tbsp (30 mL)	coarsely chopped fresh mint
1 tbsp (15 mL)	coarsely chopped coriander
2 tsp (10 mL)	minced fresh ginger
1 tbsp (15 mL)	lime juice
	Salt and pepper to taste
12 oz (375 g)	soft fresh goat cheese, at room temperature
18	slices (1/4 inch/5 mm) unpeeled seedless cucumber
1	sweet red pepper, cut into 12 strips
	Warm pita bread or pita chips

Combine tomatoes, green onions, mint, coriander and ginger. (Can be prepared up to 4 hours in advance, covered and reserved in refrigerator.) Add lime juice, salt and pepper just before serving.

Spread goat cheese over a medium-sized serving platter. Sprinkle tomato mixture over cheese. Surround with cucumber slices and pepper strips. Serve pita bread or chips on the side. Makes 6 servings.

Grilled Salmon With Dill and Mustard Seeds

Dill is a favourite seasoning for salmon; here, it's complemented by spicy mustard seeds and cumin. Mayonnaise helps the spices adhere to the salmon, adds moistness and prevents the fish from sticking to the grate.

1/4 cup (50 mL)	mayonnaise
1 tbsp (15 mL)	plain yogurt
2 tsp (10 mL)	mustard seeds
Pinch	(or to taste) cayenne pepper
1 1/2 tsp (7 mL)	ground cumin
1/2 cup (125 mL)	chopped fresh dill
3/4 tsp (4 mL)	salt
1 tbsp (15 mL)	lemon juice
6	salmon fillets (6 oz/175 g each), skin on, or 6 salmon steaks

Combine mayonnaise, yogurt, mustard seeds, cayenne, cumin, dill, salt and lemon juice in a large bowl. (Can be made several hours in advance, covered and reserved in refrigerator.) Add salmon to mayonnaise mixture and turn to coat evenly.

Preheat grill to medium-high (or preheat broiler). Grill salmon, skin side up, for 3 to 4 minutes. Turn and cook for 3 to 4 minutes longer or just until middle of salmon is opaque when pierced with small knife. Transfer to a serving platter or individual plates. Makes 6 servings.

Spiced Potato and Green-bean Salad

This dish is a zesty twist on traditional potato salad.

1 1/2 lb (750 g)	cooked red potatoes
1 lb (500 g)	green beans, cut into 3/4-inch (2 cm) pieces
2 tbsp (30 mL)	vegetable oil
1 tsp (5 mL)	mustard seeds
1/2 tsp (2 mL)	cumin seeds
1 tbsp (15 mL)	minced gingerroot
2	cloves garlic, minced
1 1/2 tsp (7 mL)	ground coriander seeds
1/4 tsp (1 mL)	turmeric
1/4 tsp (1 mL)	cayenne pepper (approx)
Pinch	ground cinnamon
1/2 tsp (2 mL)	salt
1 tbsp (15 mL)	lemon juice
3/4 cup (175 mL)	yogurt
1/4 cup (50 mL)	mayonnaise
2	green onions, thinly sliced
1 tbsp (15 mL)	coarsely chopped coriander leaves

Cut potatoes into 3/4-inch (2 cm) cubes. Meanwhile, cook beans in a pot of boiling salted water until tender-crisp, about 4 minutes. Drain; cool under cold water and drain well.

Heat oil in a large, preferably nonstick skillet set over medium-high heat. Add mustard seeds. When they pop, add cumin, ginger and garlic. Cook until ginger browns lightly. Add ground coriander, turmeric, cayenne (to taste), cinnamon and salt. Stir well, then add potatoes. Cook for 1 to 2 minutes, stirring to coat potatoes with spices. Transfer to bowl and toss with lemon juice. Let cool completely.

Combine yogurt, mayonnaise, green onions and coriander in a large bowl. Add cooled potatoes and green beans and mix well. Cover and refrigerate. Makes 6 servings.

Warm Mushroom and Spinach Salad With Fennel and Tomatoes

Although this unusual salad has a mildly licorice flavour, it is fresh and light-tasting.

4 tbsp (60 mL)	vegetable oil
1 tsp (5 mL)	fennel seeds
1	medium onion, cut in half lengthwise, then into thin slices crosswise
1 lb (500 g)	mushrooms, thinly sliced
2	medium tomatoes, finely chopped
1/2 tsp (2 mL)	ground ginger
1/4 tsp (1 mL)	turmeric
	Salt and pepper
1 lb (500 g)	spinach, stemmed, washed and dried
3 tbsp (45 mL)	lemon juice
1	clove garlic, minced

Heat 2 tbsp (30 mL) of the oil in a large skillet set over high heat. Add fennel seeds and onion. Cook, stirring frequently, until onion is lightly browned. Add mushrooms and cook, stirring frequently, until liquid evaporates and mushrooms are lightly browned. Add tomatoes, ginger and turmeric and cook until tomatoes soften. Season to taste with salt and pepper. Remove from heat. (Can be prepared to this point up to 1 hour ahead.)

Place spinach in a large serving bowl. Mix together lemon juice, remaining oil, garlic and salt and pepper to taste. Just before serving, add to spinach and toss well. Quickly reheat mushroom mixture over high heat and add to spinach. Toss well and serve immediately. Makes 6 servings.

Mango-coconut Cake With Yogurt-lime Cream

Cool tropical flavours meet warm spices in this dessert.

3 cups (750 mL)	ripe, firm mango, peeled and cut into 1/2-inch (1 cm) pieces (2 to 3 mangoes)
1 cup (250 mL)	unsweetened large-flake coconut
3/4 cup (175 mL)	packed brown sugar
2 tsp (10 mL)	grated orange peel
1/2 tsp (2 mL)	ground cinnamon
1/4 tsp (1 mL)	ground nutmeg
1 1/2 cups (375 mL)	all-purpose flour
1 cup (250 mL)	granulated sugar
2 tsp (10 mL)	baking powder
2	eggs, lightly beaten
1/2 cup (125 mL)	milk
1/4 cup (50 mL)	butter, melted and cooled
1 tsp (5 mL)	vanilla

Yogurt-lime Cream:

1 cup (250 mL)	plain yogurt
2 tsp (10 mL)	lime juice
1 tsp (5 mL)	grated lime peel
1/2 cup (125 mL)	whipping cream
2 tbsp (30 mL)	icing sugar

Preheat oven to 350F (180C). Stir together mango, coconut, brown sugar, orange peel, cinnamon and nutmeg; reserve. Mix flour, sugar and baking

powder in a large bowl. Mix eggs with milk, melted butter and vanilla in a separate bowl. Add to flour mixture and mix just until smooth (batter will be thick).

Spread batter evenly in a greased 13- x 9-inch (3 L) baking dish. Spread mango mixture evenly over batter. Bake in preheated oven for 35 to 40 minutes or until lightly browned on top and firm to the touch. Cut into squares and serve warm or at room temperature with yogurt-lime cream on the side. Makes 6 to 8 servings.

Yogurt-lime Cream:

Stir together yogurt, lime juice and peel. Whip cream and add icing sugar. Fold into yogurt mixture. (Can be covered and refrigerated for up to 2 hours before serving.)

What to Serve With Fire and Spice

A great introductory libation to this Fire and Spice menu is a glass of chilled rosé. Hot pink in colour, a dry rosé can offer all the refreshing flavours of a white wine with the structure of a red wine, allowing it to be served throughout the meal.

The pungent flavours and richness of the Goat-cheese Dip call for an equally assertive wine such as Sancerre or Sauvignon Blanc-based wine which offer contrasting acidity and vibrant citrus/herb flavours. Sancerre is also an excellent match to the Grilled Salmon and the accompanying vegetable side dishes.

For a red wine, try serving a lighter-bodied Cabernet Franc such as a Chinon. Served cool, this wine's bright berry, herb-tinged flavours and balanced acidity tame bold flavours.

Finally, try a Vidal Icewine with dessert. Its luscious sweetness, intense tropical fruit and marmalade flavours are the key to pairing with the Mango-coconut Cake.

Summer Is
for Celebrating

Summer is the time of year when weddings, anniversaries and graduation celebrations abound. Choosing to home-cater a big event may seem like a daunting task, but it can be done pleasurably with a little planning. This menu is easy to prepare, subtle and elegant, and it can be scaled up as necessary to feed a crowd, which makes it ideal for hostesses who want to do it all themselves.

MENU

Chilled Avocado Soup

Watermelon, Radish and Cucumber Salad

Poached Chicken Breasts With Parsley Sauce

Make-ahead Green and Wax Bean Bouquets

Quinoa Pilaf

Chilled Avocado Soup

For a sit-down affair, serve this soup in cups placed on lined plates. For easy service on a buffet, ladle soup into juice glasses and present them in a bowl of crushed ice.

2 tbsp (30 mL)	lemon juice
1 tsp (5 mL)	finely grated lime peel
1/2 tsp (2 mL)	ground cumin
1/4 tsp (1 mL)	each salt and white pepper
2	shallots or 1 small onion, peeled and chopped
1	clove garlic, chopped
6 cups (1.5 L)	vegetable or chicken broth
3	large, ripe avocados or 4 cups (1 L) frozen avocado purée
	Sour cream
	Lemon or lime slices

Purée lemon juice, lime peel, cumin, salt, pepper, shallots, garlic and broth in a blender or food processor until smooth. Halve each avocado and firmly hit the pit with the butt end of a chef's knife. Turn the knife 90 degrees to remove pit. Peel off skin and chop avocado flesh. Add to blender and purée until smooth. Cover tightly and chill in refrigerator until very cold. (Can be made up to 1 day ahead.)

Ladle 3/4 cup (175 mL) soup into chilled serving bowls or small glasses. Garnish with a dollop of sour cream and a thin slice of lemon or lime. Makes 10 servings.

Tip: If making ahead, taste and add extra lemon juice, if necessary, just before serving.

Watermelon, Radish and Cucumber Salad

This novel salad tastes as good as it looks and is a special, though simple, recipe that will be remembered long after the meal is over.

2 tbsp (30 mL)	champagne or red-wine vinegar
1 tsp (5 mL)	dried thyme leaves
1/2 tsp (2 mL)	Dijon mustard
1/2 tsp (2 mL)	each salt and pepper
Pinch	granulated sugar
1/2 cup (125 mL)	extra-virgin olive oil
4 cups (1 L)	diced seedless watermelon
4 cups (1 L)	chunks of seedless cucumber
2 cups (500 mL)	small halved radishes
	Boston lettuce leaves

Whisk vinegar, thyme, mustard, salt, pepper and sugar in a small bowl. Whisking, drizzle in oil until well combined (taste and add up to 1/4 tsp/1 mL granulated sugar if necessary).

Combine watermelon, cucumbers and radishes in a large bowl. (Can be prepared to this point and covered and reserved in the refrigerator for up to 6 hours.)

Drizzle dressing over salad and toss to combine just before serving. Place single lettuce leaves on individual salad plates or line a large, deep platter with enough leaves to cover. Spoon salad mixture onto leaves and serve buffet-style. Makes 10 servings.

Tip: Add even more colour by using both yellow and red watermelon.

Poached Chicken Breasts With Parsley Sauce

Served warm or cold, this dish wil appeal to guests of all ages.

1	bay leaf
1 tsp (5 mL)	whole peppercorns
1	stalk celery, chopped
1	each lemon, onion and carrot, chopped
10	skinless, boneless chicken breasts (about 4 lb/2 kg)

Parsley Sauce:

1 cup (250 mL)	each white wine and 35% whipping cream
1 tsp (5 mL)	granulated sugar
4	green onions, chopped
2	small cloves garlic, chopped
2 cups (500 mL)	lightly packed parsley leaves
1 tsp (5 mL)	lemon juice
	Salt and pepper

Combine bay leaf, peppercorns, celery, lemon, onion and carrot in a large saucepan. Add enough water to fill pan two-thirds full. Bring to a boil and simmer for 10 minutes.

Add chicken and cook for 8 to 10 minutes or until no longer pink in centre. Remove from pan using a slotted spoon and place on a platter. Cover and cool.

Parsley Sauce:

Combine white wine, cream, sugar, onions and garlic in a small saucepan. Bring to a boil and reduce to about 1 cup (250 mL), about 20 minutes. Transfer to a blender. Add parsley and lemon juice and purée until smooth. Add salt and pepper to taste.

Spoon a little parsley sauce into the centre of each serving plate. Slice each chicken breast into long strips and fan out on plate. If serving buffet-style, fan chicken strips out on a platter and serve sauce in a boat. Makes 10 servings.

Make-ahead Green and Wax Bean Bouquets

Substitute thin lengths of asparagus for the beans if your budget permits.

1 lb (500 g)	each green and yellow wax beans
1	red pepper, quartered and thinly sliced
	Chives
1/2 tsp (2 mL)	each salt and pepper
3 tbsp (45 mL)	melted butter

Trim stem ends from beans and wash under cold running water. Boil in batches in a large pot of boiling salted water for 4 to 5 minutes or until cooked but not limp. Add red pepper for last 30 seconds of cooking.

Immerse vegetables in ice-cold water until chilled. Drain well and store, tightly covered, in the refrigerator for up to 2 days. Bundle 4 or 5 beans and a strip of red pepper together. Wind a length of chive around each bundle and tie closed. Trim ends of chives if they are long or uneven.

Reheat beans by placing bundles in a bowl or saucepan and pouring boiling water over them. Drain well. Stir salt and pepper into butter. Place beans on serving plates or platter and brush butter evenly over top. Makes 10 servings.

Quinoa Pilaf

Quinoa is a tiny bead-shaped grain. Native to South America, it has an appealing, mild flavour. And because it is also high in protein, vegetarians love it. This recipe is appropriate served either hot or at room temperature, which makes it a versatile dish for entertaining on a large scale.

2 tbsp (30 mL)	butter
1	onion, peeled and finely chopped
2 tbsp (30 mL)	each balsamic vinegar and orange juice
1 tsp (5 mL)	chopped fresh thyme leaves
1 tsp (5 mL)	grated orange peel
1/2 tsp (2 mL)	salt
2 cups (500 mL)	quinoa
4 cups (1 L)	chicken broth or water
1/2 cup (125 mL)	each diced dried apricots and dried blueberries or currants
1/2 cup (125 mL)	finely chopped chives or parsley

Melt butter in a shallow saucepan or deep skillet set over medium heat. Add onion, vinegar, orange juice, thyme, orange peel and salt. Cook, stirring often, for 5 minutes.

Add quinoa and stir for 1 minute. Add broth and bring to a boil. Reduce heat and cover. Simmer for 15 to 20 minutes or until quinoa is tender. Stir in apricots, blueberries and chives. Taste and adjust seasoning if necessary.

Serve hot or at room temperature. Scoop into a ramekin or custard cup and pack lightly. Turn out onto serving plates next to the fanned strips of chicken and bundles of beans. For buffet service, place in a bowl and fluff with a fork before serving. Makes 16 servings.

Tip: If making ahead, stir blueberries into mixture just before serving.

What to Serve With Summer Is for Celebrating

Chilled Avocado Soup deserves a wine that can match its flavour and temperature. Serve a chilled glass of crisp white Pinot Grigio. To satisfy the red-wine lover, serve a chilled light dry rosé.

If you don't want to duplicate the wines for the salad course, serve a Vidal, Gewürztraminer or Riesling.

Add a festive touch to your celebration with a sparkling wine to complement the flavours of the chicken, the beans and the Quinoa Pilaf. Or, to accent the vegetable tastes in each dish, serve a medium-bodied red such as Chilean Carmenère.

Elegant Buffets

If you're entertaining a crowd, there's no doubt that a buffet is the easiest way to serve the meal. Unfortunately, a buffet can seem too pedestrian for a swish party, but that doesn't need to be the case. One way to make your buffet sensational is to rent skirted tables from a party supplier and drape lovely linen over risers of various heights set on the tables so that the food is dramatically presented at different levels.

Also key to hosting an elegant buffet party is to make sure the food is replenished often so that it remains fresh and attractive-looking. The easiest way to set up a buffet is at a long freestanding table, which will allow two lines of guests to serve themselves at once. For small groups, a round table arranged with starters and subsequent courses set out in a clockwise pattern works well. If your party is large, set up one buffet table for every 30 people to avoid crowding.

Plates should be at the beginning of the line, but incidentals such as cutlery and napkins should be the last items on the table. Glasses for wine and other beverages should be placed either on the serving tables or passed around filled with drinks once people are seated and eating.

Movable Prairie Feast

Whether you
picnic on the
terrace of a
downtown condo,
in the park down
the street or while
on a road trip,
this menu is satisfying and fun.
Many of the ingredients highlight foods popular on the Canadian
Prairies, where there is a strong picnicking tradition.

MENU

First-from-the-garden Coleslaw

Whisky-marinated Flank Steak

Onion "Jam"

Buttermilk-rosemary Biscuits

Big-sky Saskatoon-berry Streusel Tarts

First-from-the-garden Coleslaw

Naturally sweet young carrots and cabbage give this coleslaw qualities that appeal to many who normally eschew this type of salad. Moreover, the vinaigrette dressing makes it safer for packing in a cooler than traditional mayonnaise versions.

3 tbsp (45 mL)	red-wine vinegar
1 tsp (5 mL)	honey-Dijon mustard
1/2 tsp (2 mL)	dried thyme leaves
1/2 tsp (2 mL)	caraway seeds
1/4 tsp (1 mL)	each salt and pepper
1/3 cup (75 mL)	canola oil
6 cups (1.5 L)	very finely shredded young green cabbage
2 cups (500 mL)	very finely shredded carrots
1/2 cup (125 mL)	thinly sliced green onions

Whisk vinegar with mustard, thyme, caraway, salt and pepper in a large bowl. Drizzle in oil while whisking. Add cabbage, carrots and onions. Toss to combine. Taste and adjust seasoning if necessary. (Can be made up to 8 hours ahead.) Makes 8 servings.

Whisky-marinated Flank Steak

You don't have to be a cowboy to appreciate the mellow
flavour Canadian whisky adds to this affordable cut of beef.

1/2 cup (125 mL)	Canadian whisky
1/4 cup (50 mL)	orange juice
2 tbsp (30 mL)	brown sugar
1 tbsp (15 mL)	canola oil
2 tsp (10 mL)	vanilla
2 tsp (10 mL)	dried ginger
3	cloves garlic
1/4 tsp (1 mL)	hot pepper sauce
2 lb (1 kg)	flank steak (about 3/4 inch/2 cm thick)
1/2 tsp (2 mL)	each salt and pepper

Stir together whisky, orange juice, brown sugar, oil, vanilla, ginger, garlic
and hot pepper sauce. Pour over steak; cover and marinate for at least
4 hours or up to 48 hours. Remove steak from marinade and bring to
room temperature for 30 minutes. Preheat grill to medium-high. Bring
marinade to a boil and simmer until reduced by about half.

Sprinkle steak evenly with salt and pepper. Place on a lightly greased grill
and brush liberally with reduced marinade. Cook, covered, for 7 minutes.
Turn and brush with marinade. Grill for 5 to 7 minutes or until desired
doneness. Cool to room temperature. Slice very thinly against the grain.
Makes 4 to 6 servings.

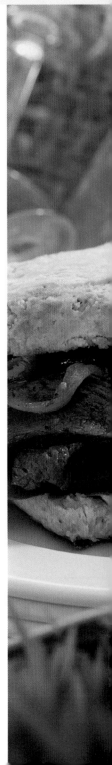

Onion "Jam"

Whether it's spread over thick slices of flank steak or used as the basis for a dip or as an add-in for mashed potatoes, this condiment has a complex, satisfying flavour.

1 tbsp (15 mL)	butter
1	each large red and white onions, peeled and sliced
1	clove garlic, minced
1 tsp (5 mL)	chopped dried sage
1/4 tsp (1 mL)	each salt and pepper
1 tbsp (15 mL)	liquid honey
2 tsp (10 mL)	cider vinegar
1/2 tsp (2 mL)	Worcestershire sauce

Melt butter in a large skillet set over medium heat. Add onions, garlic, sage, salt and pepper. Cook, stirring often, for 10 minutes or until onions are translucent. Increase heat to medium-high and cook, stirring often, for 5 minutes or until onions are just beginning to brown.

Drizzle with honey and continue to cook, stirring often, until very brown but not scorched. Add vinegar and Worcestershire sauce. Stir to scrape up any cooked-on bits. Makes 6 servings.

Buttermilk-rosemary Biscuits

While baking bread in the summer is unappealing for many busy people who don't want to warm up the house, baking biscuits is so fast and easy that you can do it in the morning as you get your gear ready for a day in the great outdoors.

4 cups (1 L)	cake and pastry flour
1/4 cup (50 mL)	finely chopped fresh rosemary
2 tsp (10 mL)	salt
4 tsp (20 mL)	baking powder
2 tsp (10 mL)	granulated sugar
1 tsp (5 mL)	baking soda
1/2 cup (125 mL)	lard or vegetable shortening
1 1/2 cups (375 mL)	buttermilk

Use a fork to stir together flour, rosemary, salt, baking powder, granulated sugar and baking soda. Cut in lard until crumbly using a pastry blender or two knives. Preheat oven to 400F (200C).

Make a well in the flour mixture and pour in buttermilk. Stir until a ragged dough forms. Turn out onto counter and knead just until dough comes together. Pat out to a 3/4-inch (2 cm) thick rectangle. Cut into 8 squares.

Transfer to an ungreased baking sheet. Bake for 15 to 18 minutes or until golden on the bottom. Cool on a rack. Makes 8 biscuits.

Big-sky Saskatoon-berry Streusel Tarts

A tribute to the heritage of Prairie bakers, these tarts are juicy but still portable, which makes them ideal for picnics. Don't forget to take along plenty of napkins, though, because Saskatoon berries can stain light-coloured fabrics.

Pastry:

3 cups (750 mL)	all-purpose flour
2 tbsp (30 mL)	granulated sugar
1/2 tsp (2 mL)	salt
3/4 cup (175 mL)	lard or vegetable shortening, cubed
1/2 cup (125 mL)	ice water

Filling:

3/4 cup (175 mL)	granulated sugar (approx)
1 tbsp (15 mL)	cornstarch
3 cups (750 mL)	thawed, drained frozen Saskatoon berries
2 tsp (10 mL)	lemon juice

Topping:

1/4 cup (50 mL)	each all-purpose flour and rolled oats
1/2 tsp (2 mL)	cinnamon
2 tbsp (30 mL)	each brown sugar and butter

Pastry:

Combine flour with sugar, salt and lard in a food processor. Blend until mixture resembles coarse crumbs. With processor running, add ice water. Turn out onto a piece of plastic wrap and press into a ball. Refrigerate for 30 minutes.

Roll out pastry and cut out twelve 3-inch (8 cm) circles. Fit into 12 muffin tins. Preheat oven to 375F (190C).

Filling:

Stir sugar with cornstarch. Sprinkle over berries and add lemon juice. Stir until evenly combined. Spoon an equal amount of filling into each tart shell.

Topping:

Combine flour, oats, cinnamon and sugar. Work butter into mixture until crumbly. Sprinkle evenly over tarts. Bake in preheated oven for 30 to 35 minutes or until pastry is golden and filling is bubbly. Cool on a rack before removing from pan. Makes 1 dozen tarts.

What to Serve With Movable Prairie Feast

First-from-the-garden Coleslaw calls for a wine that will stand up to the pungency of raw onion and cabbage. An off-dry Chenin Blanc will fill the bill.

The Whisky-marinated Flank Steak demands a wine that won't be dominated by the strong ginger, beef and smoke flavours. Baco Noir wines from Ontario can be full-bodied, and they pair well with the bold flavours of this dish. For a lighter option, go for a German or Austrian red that will deliver a burst of spicy, bright, cherry fruit flavours and a palate-cleansing finish.

An interesting match for the Saskatoon-berry Streusel Tarts is a maple liqueur. Its rich flavour and unctuous texture will work wonders with this dish. Likewise, a sweet blueberry wine offers a lively fruit character and intense blueberry notes that match the berry flavours in the tart.

Newfoundland Seafood Feast

For centuries, seafood meant cod to Newfoundlanders. The fishery dates from the time of early Basques, who harvested the waters and dried their catches on the shores of Newfoundland and Labrador as far back as 1525. With the recent decline in cod stocks, other species are now being caught, and many are being cultured with the guidance of researchers at Memorial University.

From snowy halibut, salmon and steelhead to redfish, blue mussels and king crab, the modern fishery is alive and vital. This menu featuring Newfoundland seafood has traditional roots but takes much of its inspiration from the type of cooking found in Newfoundland's better restaurants, where creativity and Atlantic bounty coalecse.

MENU

Newfoundland Mussels Asian-style

Roasted Atlantic Salmon Fillets
With Lime-begonia Butter

Summer Barley Salad

Summer-berry Crème Brûlée

Newfoundland Mussels Asian-style

The Asian flavours of lemon grass and kaffir lime leaves give steamed mussels an exotic update. Many of these ingredients can be found in local gourmet shops, and a quick trip to Chinatown will certainly stock your pantry full of the items you need for such exciting cooking.

4 lb (2 kg)	fresh mussels
2 tbsp (30 mL)	oil
2	tomatoes, diced
3	cloves garlic, minced
1 tbsp (15 mL)	minced gingerroot
1 1/2 cups (375 mL)	coconut milk
2 to 3 tsp (10 to 15 mL)	Thai green curry paste (approx)
1/2 cup (125 mL)	chopped fresh coriander leaves
2	stalks lemon grass, trimmed and cut into strips
4	kaffir lime leaves or 1 tbsp (15 mL) grated lime peel
1 tsp (5 mL)	salt
	Fresh coriander leaves

Scrub mussels and discard any that are not tightly closed. Heat oil in a large saucepan over medium heat. Add tomatoes, garlic and ginger and cook for 2 to 3 minutes to soften. Add coconut milk, curry paste, coriander, lemon grass, lime leaves and salt. Cover and bring to a boil, reduce heat and simmer for 10 minutes.

Increase heat to high. Add mussels, cover and steam for 5 minutes. Discard any mussels that do not open. Ladle into soup plates and garnish with coriander. Makes 6 servings.

Roasted Atlantic Salmon Fillets With Lime-begonia Butter

Combining the two citrusy flavours of fresh lime and organic tuberous begonia (which has a lemony taste) creates a great effect for Atlantic salmon. This salmon is also excellent grilled instead of roasted.

Lime-begonia Butter:

1/4 cup (50 mL)	butter, softened
1 tsp (5 mL)	grated lime peel
1 tsp (5 mL)	lime juice
Pinch	pepper
1 tbsp (15 mL)	shredded tuberous begonia petals (optional)

Salmon:

6	Atlantic salmon fillets (about 6 oz/175 g each)
	Canola oil
1 tbsp (15 mL)	lime juice (approx)
	Salt and pepper
	Tuberous begonia flowers

Lime-begonia Butter:

Blend butter with lime peel, juice, pepper and begonia petals in a small bowl. Cover and chill. (Alternatively, shape butter into a small log in plastic wrap and chill. Cut into slices to serve on salmon.)

Salmon:

Preheat oven to 400F (200C). Brush fillets lightly with oil. Sear fish for 45 seconds per side in a nonstick skillet set over high heat. Transfer to a lightly oiled rimmed baking sheet. Sprinkle with lime juice, salt and pepper. Roast in preheated oven until just cooked through, about 8 to 10 minutes. Serve immediately, topping each portion with a spoonful or slice of lime-begonia butter. Garnish with flowers. Makes 6 servings.

Summer Barley Salad

Inspired by Middle Eastern tabbouleh, this side-dish-style salad uses hearty and healthy Canadian barley instead of bulgur. Barley is also used in such famous Canadian concoctions as beer and whisky.

1 1/4 cups (300 mL)	pearl barley
3 cups (750 mL)	lightly salted water
1/3 cup (75 mL)	olive oil
3 tbsp (45 mL)	lemon juice
1 tsp (5 mL)	finely grated lemon peel
2	cloves garlic, minced
2	green onions, chopped
	Salt and pepper to taste
2	tomatoes, seeded and chopped
1 1/2 cups (375 mL)	diced seedless cucumber
3/4 cup (175 mL)	each chopped fresh mint and parsley
	Mint sprigs (optional)

Combine barley and water in a saucepan. Cover and bring to a boil. Reduce heat to low and simmer until barley is tender, about 25 minutes. Drain and transfer to a large bowl and toss with olive oil, lemon juice, peel, garlic, green onions, salt and pepper. Cover and chill. (Can be refrigerated for up to 2 days.)

Stir in tomatoes, cucumber, mint and parsley just before serving. Taste and adjust seasoning. Garnish with mint sprigs. Makes 6 to 8 servings.

Summer-berry Crème Brûlée

Bakeapples (known in other parts of the country as cloudberries) grow wild in Newfoundland's boggy areas; they resemble golden raspberries but are tarter tasting. Golden or red raspberries can be substituted for bakeapples and framboise for the liqueur if you can't find the cloudberry items called for in this recipe.

2 cups (500 mL)	whipping cream
³/₄ cup (175 mL)	bakeapples (cloudberries) or raspberries
1	vanilla bean, split lengthwise
6	egg yolks
¹/₂ cup (125 mL)	granulated sugar
1 tbsp (15 mL)	cloudberry liqueur
3 tbsp (45 mL)	granulated sugar for topping
	Additional berries for garnish

Preheat oven to 325F (160C). Combine cream, bakeapples and vanilla bean in a heavy saucepan. Heat gently, stirring to crush fruit lightly, until mixture begins to simmer. Remove vanilla bean. Meanwhile, beat egg yolks and sugar in a large bowl until light in colour. Whisk in liqueur and hot cream mixture. Strain through a sieve to remove seeds, pressing to extract pulp.

Divide this mixture among 6 ramekins. Place in a large roasting pan and pour in enough boiling water to come halfway up the sides of the ramekins. Place in preheated oven. Reduce heat to 300F (150C) and bake for 40 to 45 minutes or until centres are beginning to set but are still soft. Cool completely. Cover and refrigerate for at least 4 hours or up to 2 days.

Sprinkle sugar evenly over top of each cooked custard. Use a blowtorch or place under a very hot broiler to carefully caramelize sugar until bubbling and dark golden brown. Garnish with berries and serve immediately. Makes 6 servings.

Prepared in this Asian style, mussels are a perfect partner for a frosty mug of Blanche de Chambly, a unique wheat beer made in Quebec with aromas and flavours of citrus and coriander. Alternatively, serve a fragrant, soft, spicy white wine with a refreshing cut of acidity such as a Torrentés from Argentina.

Serve a white wine with a refreshing citrus palate such as Chablis with the Roasted Atlantic Salmon Fillets, or add some sparkle to this menu by popping open a bottle of dry sparkling wine. For many, the Summer Barley Salad will be served as a side dish, but others may find that it also makes a nice light meal on its own. If that's the case, try it with a glass of ice-cold Canadian ale.

Framboise liqueur is a real treat next to this special dessert for raspberry fans. An alternative is the Lakka Cloudberry liqueur from Finland, which will match the flavours very well.

Shopping for Seafood

When shopping for fish and shellfish, use all your senses to choose wisely. Look for bright gills, clear eyes and firm flesh in fish; these are key indicators of freshness. Likewise, the smell of fresh fish and shellfish should be sweet and maritime but have no hint of ammonia. Shellfish sold live such as lobster and mussels should be lively and responsive.

While choosing fish and seafood stored on ice is generally recommended over purchasing packaged and individually wrapped products, this rule may be ill advised. If you have doubts about how often the store cleans its seafood display, or if some of the fish on the ice look less than fresh, don't buy the perfect-looking shrimp displayed next to them. When seafood is stored on ice, bacteria from one item can easily contaminate all the other fish and shellfish as the ice melts. Likewise, if shellfish and fish are displayed on the same bed of ice, allergens from the shellfish could be transferred to the other items in the display case, posing a health risk for those who suffer from shellfish allergies.

Serving Wine

Needless to say, when planning a wine country dinner the wine is as important to the meal as the food itself. The rule of thumb when serving more than one wine is to change glasses for each wine to be served; if your supply of glasses is short, then rinse the glasses with a splash of water between wines.

Generally, red wine should be served at room temperature or slightly chilled (cellar temperature); it is best served in larger, balloon shaped glasses so that the wine can be swished about to open up its bouquet and flavour.

White wines are almost always best served very cold and for this reason many experts recommend keeping open bottles of white wines on ice at the table. White wine glasses are usually a little smaller than red wine glasses so that less is served at a time, thus keeping only cold wine in the glass. White wines should also always be served in glasses that have a long stem so that warm hands don't increase the temperature of the wine as the glass is held for drinking.

Bar Math

Use these facts and figures to help you to decide how much wine and liquor to purchase for your dinner party.

- A 750 mL bottle of wine = 6 servings
- Professional party planners budget one bottle of wine per person for a three or more course sit-down dinner
- 40 oz (1.18 L) bottle of liquor is enough for 25 mixed drinks

AUTUMN

Like spring, autumn stretches out across Canada at different times and at its own pace. While the mums can still be blooming in Toronto at Halloween, trick-or-treaters may be wearing snow boots in Winnipeg. Regardless of when the leaves turn colour in your hometown, fall is a wonderful time of year for cooking a big meal. Most people are back in the city after spending summer weekends at the lake or globe-trotting, and the urge to renew bonds after a busy summer is often strong.

In fact, for many people, fall is the busiest season for dinner parties. Not only does the weather offer comfortable temperatures for cooking, but the crisp, cooler days spur appetites, and the bounty of the harvest can't help but inspire delicious, gooey fruit pies and wonderful-smelling roasted dishes. This is the time of year to pull on a sweater and take a brisk walk to work up a robust appetite!

A Sunday drive to the country to visit a farmer's market for pumpkins, squash, corn, sweet peppers, eggplant, apples and pears is an autumn ritual for many, so this chapter features recipes that you can make when you come home laden with your autumn treasures.

In most cases, these fall menus highlight roasting or slow-simmering techniques that busy people often eschew during warmer weather or on hectic weeknights. These are menus for the weekend, designed for times when you can take your time over dinner. That doesn't mean these recipes are hard to prepare; on the contrary, the preparation times are just as fast as for other *Homemaker's* recipes, but in some cases, the cooking time will be longer to produce the rich, full flavours we associate with this season.

Fall entertaining can be as homey or as elegant as you'd like it to be. With the shorter days, candles are perfect for adding sparkle to either linen-swathed tables or rustic, time-worn harvest tables adorned with simple runners. Dress it up or dress it down, but do remember to incorporate the gorgeous oranges, reds and golds of the season into the centerpieces, linens and dishes you choose for fall dinner parties.

Thanksgrilling

Grilling the Thanksgiving turkey may not be traditional, but it's an excellent way to enjoy a beautiful fall day with family and friends. This menu, which is as colourful as it is delicious, combines dishes that can be made ahead with new twists on traditional favourites. So break tradition yet keep everyone happy with this novel way to approach a festive Thanksgiving meal.

MENU

Grilled Cranberry-glazed Turkey

Savoury Sage Bread Pudding

Maple-pecan Butternut Squash Wedges

Spiced Pumpkin Layer Cake With
Molasses Cream-cheese Frosting

Grilled Cranberry-glazed Turkey

A turkey cooked on the grill is moist and flavourful, and when it's glazed with cranberries, there's no need to worry about putting a dish of cranberry sauce on the table.

1 cup (250 mL)	jellied cranberry sauce
1/2 cup (125 mL)	orange juice
3 tbsp (45 mL)	finely chopped rosemary
2 tbsp (30 mL)	Dijon mustard
1 tbsp (15 mL)	Worcestershire sauce
2	cloves garlic, minced
12 lb (5.5 kg)	fresh or thawed frozen turkey
1/4 cup (50 mL)	melted butter or vegetable oil
2 tsp (10 mL)	each salt and pepper

Combine cranberry sauce with orange juice in a small saucepan. Stir in rosemary, mustard, Worcestershire sauce and garlic. Bring to a boil; reserve.

Remove giblets and neck from inside of turkey and rinse turkey inside and out with cold running water. Pat dry with paper towel. Brush all over with melted butter and sprinkle evenly with salt and pepper. Bend wings under turkey and truss legs together with cooking twine.

Preheat barbecue on high heat for 10 minutes. Reduce heat according to manufacturer's instructions to create indirect heat (on most barbecues, this will mean turning off one side or the front burner and cooking on the cooler area). Turn temperature of any burners that remain on to high or to a setting that maintains an internal barbecue temperature of approximately 300F (150C) when the lid is closed. Place a drip pan below the grate of the barbecue.

Place unstuffed turkey, breast up, on the greased cooking grate over the drip pan. Close lid and cook for 1 hour. Brush cranberry mixture evenly all over turkey. Turn turkey 90 degrees. Continue cooking, basting occasionally and rotating 90 degrees every hour, until internal temperature of the body near the inner leg is 180F (82C) and breast temperature is 170F (77C) on an instant-read meat thermometer. Overall cooking time should be about 3 1/2 to 4 hours.

Remove turkey from grill by sliding it onto a rimmed baking sheet using oven mitts or heavy-duty metal spatulas. Let stand for 20 minutes before carving. Makes 12 hearty servings.

Savoury Sage Bread Pudding

This casserole is an ideal accompaniment to turkey, and when made with vegetable broth, it will stand as a tasty entrée for any vegetarians at your festive table.

2 tbsp (30 mL)	vegetable oil
1	onion, peeled and chopped
1	stalk celery, finely chopped
1/2 tsp (2 mL)	each salt and pepper
1	clove garlic, minced
1 1/2 tsp (7 mL)	dried crumbled sage or 1 tbsp (15 mL) chopped fresh sage
2 cups (500 mL)	sliced mushrooms
4 cups (1 L)	cubed day-old bread
3	eggs, beaten
1 1/2 cups (375 mL)	vegetable or chicken broth
2	green onions, thinly sliced

Heat half the oil in a skillet set over medium-low heat. Add onion, celery, salt, pepper, garlic and sage and cook, stirring occasionally, for 5 minutes. Increase heat to medium-high. Add remaining oil, then mushrooms. Cook, tossing, for 3 to 4 minutes or until browned.

Preheat oven to 350F (180C). Lightly oil a 10-inch (25 cm) pie plate or shallow casserole dish. Spread bread cubes evenly in dish. Sprinkle with onion mixture. Whisk eggs into broth and pour evenly over bread mixture. Sprinkle green onions on top. (Can be prepared to this point, covered and refrigerated overnight. Bring to room temperature for 30 minutes before cooking.)

Bake in centre of preheated oven for about 40 minutes or until set and golden. Let rest for 10 minutes before slicing and serving. Makes 8 to 10 servings.

Maple-pecan Butternut Squash Wedges

Divinely sweet and smoky, this dish will convert anyone who speculated about the appropriateness of grilling Thanksgiving dinner.

2	acorn or pepper squashes (about 3 lb/1.5 kg)
1/4 cup (50 mL)	maple syrup
2 tbsp (30 mL)	butter, melted
2 tsp (10 mL)	finely grated orange peel
1/2 tsp (2 mL)	minced gingerroot
1/2 tsp (2 mL)	each salt and pepper
1/4 cup (50 mL)	chopped toasted pecans

Wash squash and cut in half. Remove seeds and cut each half into 5 wedges. Boil in a large pot of salted water for 7 minutes or until yellow flesh is almost fork-tender. (Can be prepared to this point, covered and refrigerated for up to 2 days.)

Combine syrup with butter, orange peel, ginger, salt and pepper. Preheat grill to medium-high or oven to 375F (190C). Place squash, skin side down, on grill.

Brush with maple mixture and cook, turning to prevent scorching, for 10 minutes. Brush again with glaze and turn onto one side. Cook for 5 minutes. Turn and cook for 5 minutes longer. Brush all over with remaining glaze.

Sprinkle pecans over cooked squash just before serving. (If not grilling, roast parboiled squash in oven, basting often, for 20 to 30 minutes or until tender.) Makes 8 to 10 servings.

Tip: Can be made ahead and reheated just before serving.

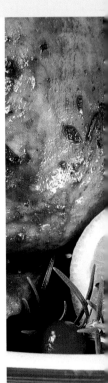

Spiced Pumpkin Layer Cake With Molasses Cream-cheese Frosting

Despite its impressive four tiers, this moist spiced pumpkin cake is quite simple to make. A nice change from pumpkin pie, it still bows to tradition by using pumpkin and Thanksgiving flavours.

2 cups (500 mL)	all-purpose flour
2 tsp (10 mL)	baking powder
1 tsp (5 mL)	baking soda
1 tsp (5 mL)	salt
2 tsp (10 mL)	cinnamon
1 cup (250 mL)	vegetable oil
2 cups (500 mL)	granulated sugar
4	eggs
2 cups (500 mL)	puréed unsweetened pumpkin
2	packages (8 oz /250 g each) brick-style cream cheese, softened
3 tbsp (45 mL)	fancy molasses
3 cups (750 mL)	icing sugar

Stir together flour, baking powder, baking soda, salt and cinnamon; reserve. Preheat oven to 350F (180C). Grease two 9-inch (1.5 L) round cake pans.

Combine oil and sugar using an electric mixer; mix on medium speed for 1 minute. Still mixing, add eggs one at a time. Increase speed to high and beat for 2 minutes. Add dry ingredients in 3 additions, scraping down bowl with a rubber spatula after each addition. Stir in pumpkin.

Scrape an equal amount of batter into each cake pan. Bake in preheated oven for 30 to 35 minutes or until a tester inserted into centre comes out clean. Cool in pan for 5 minutes, remove and cool to room temperature on rack.

Beat cream cheese with electric mixer until smooth. Add molasses and half the icing sugar. Mix on low speed until combined. Add remaining sugar and mix until combined. Increase speed to high and beat for 1 minute or until very smooth.

Cut each cake layer in half to make four layers. Spread just enough frosting over bottom layer to cover well. Repeat with second and third layers. Top with last layer and remaining frosting, swirling frosting to decorate. Makes 8 to 10 servings.

What to Serve With Thanksgrilling

The complex range of flavours that blend together to create this delicious Thanksgiving meal calls for versatile yet flavourful wines. From the fruit flavours in the turkey to the maple syrup in the squash, this menu requires a wine with good acidity and strong fruit character such as a dry Riesling. For the red-wine lover, try a cranberry wine, which will compliment the cranberry glaze while adding just a hint of spice.

The rich Spiced Pumpkin Layer Cake calls for a delicate drink that will work with it rather than compete with it. Try a Pineau des Charentes, a vin de liqueur produced in France by blending Cognac with grape juice to create a sweet, complex dessert elixir. Or highlight the cake's flavours with an Orange Muscat; the honeyed orange tones will balance the cinnamon and molasses while providing an additional fruit dimension.

Indian Summer Celebration

Enjoy the final
glorious days
of autumn with a
comfortable country-style
feast of late-harvest ingredients.
This easy all-in-one-oven
menu would also make
a lovely Thanksgiving dinner.
Each dish makes eight
generous servings,
so this is a
crowd-pleasing meal.

MENU

Mulled Cranberry Cider

Carrot and Fennel Salad With Nuts and Seeds

Cinnamon-roasted Chicken

Baked Autumn Vegetables With Barley
and Wild Rice

Pear-apricot Tarte

Mulled Cranberry Cider

With its lovely colour, fragrance and tart-sweet flavour, this is very enjoyable for pre-dinner sipping. Fresh ginger adds a pleasant bit of heat.

3 cups (750 mL)	cranberry juice
3 cups (750 mL)	apple cider
1 tbsp (15 mL)	grated gingerroot
1 tsp (5 mL)	whole allspice (or 1/2 tsp/2 mL ground allspice)

Combine cranberry juice, cider, ginger and allspice in a large saucepan. Cover and bring slowly to a boil over medium heat. Reduce heat to low and simmer for 45 minutes. Strain and serve hot. Makes 6 cups (1.5 L).

Carrot and Fennel Salad With Nuts and Seeds

Crunchy nuts and seeds top off a make-ahead combo of shredded vegetables and apples. Fennel (sometimes called anise) is available in most supermarkets. Use the feathery leaves in green salads or as a garnish in place of herbs.

1/2 tsp (2 mL)	vegetable oil
1/2 cup (125 mL)	coarsely chopped skinned hazelnuts or blanched almonds
1/2 cup (125 mL)	shelled sunflower seeds
1	large fennel bulb
4 cups (1 L)	shredded carrots
1	unpeeled apple, cored and diced

2	green onions, chopped
	Apple slices dipped in lemon juice, green onion curls
	or fennel leaves

Dressing:

1/3 cup (75 mL)	cider vinegar
1/4 cup (50 mL)	vegetable oil
2 tbsp (30 mL)	granulated sugar
1/2 tsp (2 mL)	salt

Drizzle oil into a large skillet set over medium-high heat. Add chopped nuts and sunflower seeds. Stir until lightly toasted; reserve.

Trim fennel bulb, removing leaves. With a large, sharp knife, cut bulb into thin shreds (you should have about 2 cups/500 mL). Combine fennel, carrots, apple and green onions in a large bowl.

Dressing:

Combine vinegar, oil, sugar and salt, whisking until sugar is dissolved. Pour over vegetables and toss. (Salad may be covered and refrigerated for up to 8 hours.) Just before serving, stir all but 2 tbsp (30 mL) of the toasted nuts and seeds into salad. Sprinkle remaining nuts and seeds on top. Garnish with apple slices, green onions or fennel leaves. Makes 8 to 10 servings.

Hazelnuts

Hazelnuts (also called filberts) grow in clusters on hazelnut trees in Mediterranean countries such as Turkey, Italy and France. Hazelnuts are usually sold with the brown skin on, although skinned hazelnuts are available at some bulk-food stores. Unfortunately, the skin covering the hazelnut meat is bitter and needs to be removed before baking or cooking. To remove skins, place hazelnuts on a baking sheet in a preheated 350F (180C) oven for 10 to 15 minutes or until skin begins to flake and crack open. Wrap handfuls of hot nuts in a kitchen towel and remove skins by rubbing nuts against one another and the towel.

Cinnamon-roasted Chicken

Chicken pieces are easier and faster to roast than a large bird; for best flavour and moistness, choose high-quality plump chickens or a capon. The cinnamon-scented seasoning adds a deliciously different touch and creates a delectable aroma all over the house.

2	roasting chickens (about 4.5 lb/2 kg each)
	or
1	capon (about 9 lb/4 kg)
2 tsp (10 mL)	cinnamon
1 tsp (5 mL)	dried thyme
1 tsp (5 mL)	salt
1/2 tsp (2 mL)	pepper

Preheat oven to 375F (190C). Cut chicken into serving-size pieces using poultry shears or a large, sharp knife. Mix together cinnamon, thyme, salt and pepper. Rub mixture all over the surface of the chicken pieces. Arrange pieces, skin side up and slightly apart in a single layer, in a large, nonstick or lightly greased baking pan (or 2 smaller pans).

Roast in preheated oven, basting occasionally with pan drippings, for 1 hour or until an instant-read meat thermometer registers 180F (82C) when the thickest portion is pierced and skin is crisp and browned. (If you prefer not to eat the skin, the meat is still well flavoured with the seasoning.) Makes 8 to 10 servings.

Baked Autumn Vegetables With Barley and Wild Rice

Vegetables and grains cook conveniently together in this big savoury casserole. You can use any combination of your preferred vegetables as long as the total amount equals about 8 cups (2 L). Save any leftovers for toting in your lunch box.

1 cup (250 mL)	wild rice
1/4 cup (50 mL)	butter
2 cups (500 mL)	chopped onions
1 cup (250 mL)	pearl barley
2 cups (500 mL)	each sweet potatoes, squash, parsnips and celeriac/celery root, peeled and cut into large, bite-size chunks
1 lb (500 g)	mushrooms, halved or quartered if large (optional)
1 tsp (5 mL)	salt
1/4 tsp (1 mL)	pepper
3 cups (750 mL)	chicken broth
1 cup (250 mL)	apple cider

Rinse wild rice in a strainer under cold running water. Place in a saucepan, add 4 cups (1 L) water, cover and bring to a boil. Reduce heat and boil gently for 10 minutes. Drain and reserve.

Preheat oven to 375F (190C). Melt butter over medium heat in a large skillet. Add onions and cook until softened. Stir in barley and wild rice. Transfer mixture to a 16-cup (4 L) baking dish or roasting pan. Spread vegetables and mushrooms (if using) over grains. Sprinkle with salt and pepper. Pour in chicken broth and cider. Cover with lid or foil. Bake in preheated oven for 60 to 75 minutes or until barley and rice are tender (the rice should be slightly chewy). Makes 8 to 12 servings.

Pear-apricot Tarte

Featuring an easy pat-in crust, this rustic dessert is filled with a sumptuous blend of Bosc pears, dried apricots, yogurt and brown sugar. Serve it warm in small wedges with a scoop of good-quality vanilla ice cream.

1 cup (250 mL)	sliced dried apricots
1/2 cup (125 mL)	apple cider

Crust:

1/2 cup (125 mL)	butter
1/4 cup (50 mL)	granulated sugar
1 1/4 cups (300 mL)	all-purpose flour

Filling:

3	large Bosc pears, peeled and thinly sliced
1/3 cup (75 mL)	plain yogurt
2 tbsp (30 mL)	milk

Topping:

1/2 cup (125 mL)	packed brown sugar
2 tbsp (30 mL)	all-purpose flour
2 tbsp (30 mL)	butter

Combine apricots and cider in a small saucepan. Cover and bring to a boil; reduce heat and simmer for 3 minutes. Remove from heat and let cool while making crust.

Crust:

Preheat oven to 375F (190C). Cream butter with granulated sugar. Add flour and blend until mixture is crumbly. Press evenly into bottom and halfway up sides of a 10-inch (25 cm) flan pan with removable base. Bake in preheated oven for 10 to 15 minutes or until light golden in colour. Remove from oven.

Filling:

Spread apricots evenly over crust. Arrange pear slices, slightly over-lapping, on top. Mix yogurt with milk and drizzle over pears.

Topping:

Stir together brown sugar and flour. Add butter and blend with fork until crumbly. Sprinkle over filling. Bake in 375F (190C) oven for 40 minutes or until pears are tender. Let cool on rack. Makes 12 servings.

What to Serve With Indian Summer Celebration

Indian summer is a great time to contemplate the fall colours and mild weather. Festive colours and savoury flavours highlight these dishes. The main plate of cinnamon chicken, the carrot and fennel salad and the baked vegetables have a wide variety of flavours. Wine with personality is called for. Those who prefer a white wine would do well with a Muscat from Alsace. The bright fruity flavours and full body of the wine will complement the spices and flavours of the dishes. An alternative would be a Grüner-Veltliner from Austria. The crispness and white pepper notes in the wine will bring out the herb and spice flavours in the chicken.

Red wine drinkers will enjoy a fruity red with character. A Valpolicella *Ripasso* would fit the bill wonderfully with its rich fruit and silky texture. The *Ripasso* method adds body and flavour to the wine that enhance its overall taste. The nuts, seeds and fennel in the salad will also bring out some of the complex flavours in the wine.

A natural for dessert is the Cave Spring "Indian Summer" Riesling. It is a Late Harvest Riesling with the perfect name for this meal. If this wine is not available, a good Canadian or German Late Harvest wine would enhance the flavours of the Pear-apricot Tarte.

Taste of the Country

Canadian rural areas such as Prince Edward County on the north shore of eastern Lake Ontario are wonderful to visit in the autumn, when fall fairs featuring local crafts and produce are held. With fall colours to enjoy as well as a chance to purchase seasonal bounty such as apples, pumpkins, corn, beets and sweet potatoes, driving to the country becomes a compelling way to work up an appetite.

MENU

Pumpkin and Sweet-potato Soup

Cider-glazed Pork Chops With Apple,
Corn and Herb Stuffing

Roasted Beet and Barley Risotto

Love-apple Salad

Lemon-geranium Pound Cake

Pumpkin and Sweet-potato Soup

Subtly spiced and just sweet enough, this creamy-textured soup is quick to prepare.

1/4 cup (50 mL)	butter or vegetable oil
1 lb (500 g)	diced peeled pumpkin or butternut squash (about 2 cups/500 mL)
2	medium sweet potatoes, peeled and diced
1	medium onion, diced
2	cloves garlic, minced
1 tbsp (15 mL)	minced gingerroot
1 tsp (5 mL)	chopped fresh thyme
1/4 cup (50 mL)	orange juice concentrate
8 cups (2 L)	chicken or rich vegetable broth
1/2 cup (125 mL)	cream or milk (optional)
	Salt and pepper
1 tbsp (15 L)	finely grated orange peel

Melt butter in a large pot set over medium heat. Add pumpkin, sweet potatoes and onion and cook, stirring often, for 5 to 10 minutes, until slightly softened. Add garlic, ginger, thyme, orange juice and broth. Bring to a boil, reduce heat, cover and simmer for about 30 minutes or until vegetables are soft.

Blend until smooth in batches, using a food processor or blender. Return to pot and stir in cream, if using. Season with salt and pepper to taste and stir in orange peel. Makes 6 to 8 servings.

Cider-glazed Pork Chops With Apple, Corn and Herb Stuffing

Cunningly filled with a savoury mixture of fresh fall apples and corn, this approach to pork chops is special enough to serve at a fancy occasion.

2 tbsp (30 mL)	vegetable oil
1	small onion, diced
1/2 cup (125 mL)	corn kernels scraped from fresh cob
2	Empire or Spartan apples, peeled and diced
3	cloves garlic, minced
1/2 cup (125 mL)	dry apple cider
1/3 cup (75 mL)	chicken broth
1 tbsp (15 mL)	each chopped fresh parsley, sage and thyme (or 1 tsp/5 mL dried)
6	pork loin chops (about 7 oz/200 g each and 1 inch/2.5 cm thick)

Cider Glaze:

2 tsp (10 mL)	butter
2 tbsp (30 mL)	minced shallots
2/3 cup (150 mL)	dry white wine
1 cup (250 mL)	apple cider
2 tsp (10 mL)	cider vinegar
	Salt and pepper to taste
	apple slices
	fresh sage

Heat 1 tbsp (15 mL) of the oil in a medium skillet over medium-high heat. Add onion, corn, apples and half the garlic; cook until slightly softened. Add cider and broth; boil gently until reduced by half. Stir in parsley, sage and thyme; reserve.

Preheat oven to 450F (230C). Cut a pocket in each pork chop. Spoon stuffing into pockets and fasten each with one or two toothpicks. Heat remaining oil over medium-high heat in a large, heavy ovenproof skillet (if handle is not ovenproof, wrap in foil). Place chops in skillet and spread remaining garlic on top of each. Sear chops on underside only and turn over when nicely browned.

Place skillet in preheated oven for 10 to 15 minutes or until chops are cooked through. Remove toothpicks. Transfer chops to heated platter and cover with foil to keep warm.

Cider Glaze:

Discard accumulated fat from the pork-chop skillet. Place skillet over medium-high heat and add butter. Cook shallots until softened. Add wine, stirring to deglaze pan, and cook until the wine is slightly reduced. Add cider and reduce again by one-third. Stir in vinegar, salt and pepper. To serve, spoon glaze over chops. Garnish with apple and fresh sage. Makes 6 servings.

Roasted Beet and Barley Risotto

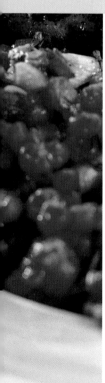

Versatile barley substitutes for rice in this satisfying version of the Italian classic. The sweet flavours of thyme, allspice and beets are perfect foils for the toasty-tasting barley.

2	medium beets
2 tbsp (30 mL)	lemon juice
2 tbsp (30 mL)	vegetable oil
1	medium onion, diced
2	medium carrots, diced
2	cloves garlic, minced
3	whole allspice, crushed (or 1/4 tsp/1 mL ground)
1 cup (250 mL)	pearl barley
1 cup (250 mL)	sliced mushrooms

3 cups (750 mL)	hot chicken broth or apple juice (approx)
1 tbsp (15 mL)	chopped fresh thyme
2	green onions, sliced
2 tbsp (30 mL)	chopped fresh parsley
	Salt and pepper

Preheat oven to 350F (180C). Wrap beets loosely in foil and roast for 1 hour or until tender when pierced. Peel and dice beets; mix with lemon juice and reserve.

Heat oil in a large skillet set over medium-high heat. Add onion, carrots, garlic and allspice. Cook, stirring, until vegetables are softened. Add barley and mushrooms and continue to cook, stirring, until lightly browned. Add broth and thyme. Bring to a boil.

Transfer to an 8-cup (2 L) baking dish. Cover and bake in preheated oven for 30 to 40 minutes or until barley is tender, adding more liquid if required. Gently stir in beets, green onions and parsley. Add salt and pepper to taste. Makes 6 servings.

Love-apple Salad

"Love-apple" is a now seldom-used but still poetic name for tomato. In this salad, succulent late-harvest tomatoes are combined with apples and broccolini and dressed for success with a balsamic-based vinaigrette.

4	broccolini stalks or 1 small head broccoli
1	Cortland apple, diced
1/2	red onion, thinly sliced
8	cherry tomatoes, quartered

1/3 cup (75 mL)	dry apple cider
2 tbsp (30 mL)	balsamic vinegar
1/2 cup (125 mL)	chopped parsley
	Salt and pepper to taste

Cut broccolini into thin slices or broccoli into small florets. Blanch in boiling water for 1 to 2 minutes or until bright green and slightly softened. Drain and refresh in cold water; drain well.

Combine broccolini, apple, red onion and cherry tomatoes in a serving bowl. Stir together cider, vinegar and parsley. Toss with vegetables. Taste and season with salt and pepper as desired. Makes 6 servings.

Lemon-geranium Pound Cake

This floral-scented teacake is typical of the type of loaves rural ladies used to bake for community sales and to serve to drop-in visitors.

6	lemon geranium leaves (unsprayed, clean and dry)
2 cups (500 mL)	all-purpose flour
2 tsp (10 mL)	baking powder
1 tsp (5 mL)	salt
1/4 tsp (1 mL)	freshly grated nutmeg
1/2 cup (125 mL)	unsalted butter
1 cup (250 mL)	granulated sugar
	Grated peel of 1 lemon
5	eggs, separated
1/2 cup (125 mL)	milk
2 tbsp (30 mL)	granulated sugar
1 tbsp (15 mL)	finely grated lemon peel

Glaze:

| 1/4 cup (50 mL) | each lemon juice and granulated sugar |

Preheat oven to 325F (160C). Press 3 of the geranium leaves into the bottom of a greased 9- x 5-inch (2 L) loaf pan; reserve. Sift together flour, baking powder, salt and nutmeg; reserve. Cream butter in a large bowl. Gradually add sugar and lemon peel, beating until light. Add egg yolks, one at a time, beating well after each addition. Stir in flour mixture alternately with milk.

Beat egg whites to soft peaks. Gradually beat in 2 tbsp (30 mL) sugar, beating to stiff peaks. Fold whites into batter. Turn batter into prepared pan and spread evenly. Bake in preheated oven for 60 to 70 minutes or until tester inserted in centre comes out clean. Let cool slightly in pan.

Glaze:

Combine lemon juice and sugar in a small saucepan. Boil gently until slightly thickened, about 4 minutes. Remove cake from pan. Brush glaze over top and press geranium leaves into glaze to make a pattern down the centre of the cake. Makes about 20 slices.

What to Serve With Taste of the Country

Serve Gewürztraminer with a hint of sweetness and a floral, fruity nose with the Pumpkin and Sweet-potato Soup. You could also serve a fruity unoaked Australian Chardonnay, with a clean finish.

Cider-glazed Pork Chops with Apple, Corn and Herb Stuffing is a versatile dish that is easy to match. Cider will maintain the fall apple theme, while white-wine fans should look to Spain, where the whites have inviting summer fruit aromas balanced with a crisp finish. Or serve a red wine such as Lemberger, with hints of strawberry and light cherry on the nose, soft tannins and a clean finish.

If you're a fan of lemon, be sure to try a chilled glass of Italian Lemoncello with the cake while the coffee is brewing.

A Cabin-Weekend Feast

What could be better before winter hits than getting out of the city with friends to enjoy fall colours, good company and good food?

If the thought of preparing a meal that takes seven hours to cook scares you, think again. Slow-cooking couldn't be easier. In fact, it makes enjoying the last rays of fall sunshine with friends easier than you ever imagined. While you're outdoors, dinner very slowly simmers, virtually cooking itself. So invite some pals over, take a trek through the woods and walk away from dinner!

MENU

Oven-barbecued Brisket

Moroccan Spiced Baked Beans

Fall Greens With Roasted Tomatoes

Warm Spiced Apple Cider

Pear-cranberry Crumble

Oven-barbecued Brisket

Southern-style pit barbecues produce tender, juicy meat that literally falls apart. This oven version adds Asian influences and produces a hearty main course that's a perfect choice after you work up an appetite hiking or raking leaves.

4 lb (2 kg)	beef brisket
2 tbsp (30 mL)	all-purpose flour
1/2 tsp (2 mL)	each salt and pepper
2 tbsp (30 mL)	vegetable oil
1	large onion, chopped
2	cloves garlic, minced
1/2 tsp (2 mL)	ground allspice
1/4 cup (50 mL)	maple syrup
1 tbsp (15 mL)	minced gingerroot
1 cup (250 mL)	each red wine and apple juice or apple cider
1/4 cup (50 mL)	hoisin sauce
1 tbsp (15 mL)	lime juice
8	fluffy white buns

Preheat oven to 275F (140C). Using a paper towel, pat the brisket dry. Mix the flour with salt and pepper, then dredge brisket in flour mixture. In a large covered casserole or Dutch oven, heat oil over medium-high heat. Add the brisket and brown on both sides. Remove to a platter.

Reduce heat to medium and add onion. Cook, stirring occasionally, for 5 minutes. Add garlic, allspice, maple syrup and ginger. Cook, stirring often, for 5 minutes longer. Stir in wine, apple juice and hoisin sauce. Bring to a boil, then return the brisket and any collected juices to the pan. Cover pan tightly and place in preheated oven. Cook for 6 hours or until meat is very tender. Remove meat from pan and tent loosely with foil.

Increase heat to medium-high and bring juices to a boil. Boil hard for 10 minutes or until thickened. Stir in lime juice. Remove fat cap from meat and discard. Using two forks, shred the brisket and pile meat onto fluffy white buns. Top with sauce.

Moroccan Spiced Baked Beans

Although aromatic and fully flavoured, the sauce for these beans is slightly astringent and only vaguely sweet, giving this high-fibre recipe broad appeal, so even if you normally eschew baked beans, try these.

2 1/2 cups (625 mL)	dried northern or navy beans or black-eyed peas
2 tsp (10 mL)	vegetable oil
3	strips of bacon, diced
1	onion, diced
1	each large green and red peppers
3	cloves garlic, minced
1	jalapeño pepper, seeded and chopped, or 1 tsp (5 mL) jalapeño sauce
2 tbsp (30 mL)	brown sugar
1 tbsp (15 mL)	cumin
1 tsp (5 mL)	salt
1 tsp (5 mL)	each ground cardamom, coriander seeds and cinnamon
2	cans (28 oz/796 mL each) chopped tomatoes
1 cup (250 mL)	water
1 tbsp (15 mL)	Dijon mustard
1/4 cup (50 mL)	chopped fresh coriander leaves

Rinse beans well and place in a large bowl. Cover with 8 cups (2 L) cold water and let stand overnight. Drain and rinse well. Alternatively, place rinsed beans in a large saucepan with 8 cups (2 L) water. Bring to a boil and reduce heat. Simmer for 5 minutes. Remove from heat and let stand for 1 hour. Drain and rinse well.

Preheat oven to 275F (140C). Set a Dutch oven or other ovenproof pan with a tight-fitting lid over medium heat. Add the oil and bacon and cook, stirring often, for 10 minutes or until bacon is crisp. Pour off all except 1 tbsp (15 mL) fat. Add the onion and cook for 5 minutes until softened. Meanwhile, quarter the peppers. Remove the seeds and white ribs and chop finely. Add peppers, garlic, jalapeño, brown sugar, cumin, salt, cardamom, coriander seeds and cinnamon.

Remove from heat and stir in tomatoes, all their juices, water, mustard and reserved beans. Cover tightly and place in preheated oven. Bake for 7 hours. Stir in coriander leaves. Makes 8 servings.

Fall Greens With Roasted Tomatoes

Inspired by the colours of fall leaves, this salad makes a pretty centrepiece for a late-harvest dinner menu. If you don't feel like roasting the tomatoes, try to find grape tomatoes, which are intensely flavoured and will add a nice depth to this salad even when added raw.

2 tbsp (30 mL)	balsamic vinegar
2 tsp (10 mL)	dried thyme leaves
1/2 tsp (2 mL)	Dijon mustard
1 tsp (5 mL)	granulated sugar
1/2 tsp (2 mL)	each salt and pepper
1/2 cup (125 mL)	olive oil
1	container (2 cups /500 mL) each red and yellow cherry tomatoes, hulls removed, and halved
7 cups (1.75 L)	peppery greens such as shredded endive, radicchio and arugula

Preheat oven to 275F (140C). Whisk vinegar with thyme, mustard, sugar, salt and pepper in a small bowl. Whisking constantly, drizzle in olive oil. Place tomatoes in a bowl and toss with half the dressing. Spread evenly on a rimmed baking sheet and place in preheated oven below baking beans. Roast for 40 minutes until shrivelled but still soft. Cool completely.

Wash greens and tear into bite-size pieces. Place in a large bowl. Just before serving, add tomatoes to greens. Stir remaining dressing and drizzle over salad. Toss gently to combine. Makes 8 servings.

Warm Spiced Apple Cider

This warming drink is great to serve when you return home from a walk or to take along in a Thermos.

8 cups (2 L)	apple cider or juice
1/2 tsp (2 mL)	whole cloves
3	4-inch (10 cm) cinnamon sticks
3	star anise (optional)
1	long strip orange peel

Combine cider, cloves, cinnamon sticks, star anise (if using) and orange peel in a large saucepan. Bring to a boil. Reduce heat and simmer for 5 minutes. Keep warm over very low heat. Makes 8 servings.

Pear-cranberry Crumble

This rustic crumble can be made up to a day ahead, but be careful, it may be hard to resist at breakfast time.

8	pears, peeled, cored and sliced
1 cup (250 mL)	dried cranberries
1/3 cup (75 mL)	granulated sugar
2 tbsp (30 mL)	all-purpose flour
2 tsp (10 mL)	finely grated lemon peel
1 tsp (5 mL)	each cinnamon and ginger
3/4 cup (175 mL)	each all-purpose flour and quick-cooking rolled oats
2/3 cup (150 mL)	lightly packed brown sugar
1/2 cup (125 mL)	melted butter
	Vanilla ice cream (optional)

Preheat oven to 350F (180C) and lightly butter a 13- x 9-inch (3 L) baking pan. Stir together pears, cranberries, sugar, 2 tbsp (30 mL) flour, lemon peel, cinnamon and ginger. Place in prepared baking dish.

Stir together 3/4 cup (175 mL) flour, oats and brown sugar in a bowl using a fork. Drizzle butter over flour mixture and toss until mixture is crumbly. Sprinkle evenly over fruit.

Bake in centre of preheated oven for 55 to 60 minutes or until topping is golden and pears are tender. Serve warm with a scoop of vanilla ice cream. Makes 8 servings.

What to Serve With A Cabin-Weekend Feast

Taking time to relax and enjoy yourself while savouring the wonderful fall flavours in these recipes calls for drinks that match the mood. Why not begin dinner with an aperitif such as a chilled glass of Tawny Port from Portugal or Fino Sherry from Spain? Serve in small, chimney-shaped glasses called *copitas* for supreme authenticity.

Brisket usually calls for red wine, something bold and flavourful but soft enough that it doesn't conflict with the Asian spices in this recipe. Try blended Cabernet-Merlot wines from British Columbia, which are elegant wines packed with fruit. White-wine fans should opt for a similar profile — full-flavoured yet soft. A favourite is Gewürztraminer for a perfumed floral explosion, or try a Riesling, with pretty citrus, pear and honeyed aromas and flavours.

With the Pear-cranberry Crumble, indulge in a Late Harvest Vidal from Ontario. Rich pear, apricot and baked peach aromas and flavours will match very well with the fruit and crumbled topping.

La Belle Cuisine

After a busy week of grabbing what you can for dinner, a traditional Sunday spread really hits the spot. This Quebec-inspired menu celebrates fall with rustic dishes that combine many of the ingredients and flavours for which *la belle province* is famous. While several of the dishes can be prepared at least partially in advance, taking a couple of hours to prepare this hearty dinner is a pleasure in itself!

MENU

Gaspé Oyster and Apple Soup

Cider-raisin Glazed Pork Loin Roast

Cauliflower and Oka Skillet Soufflé

Brussels Sprout Leaves in Whisky-orange
Sauce

Blueberry White-chocolate Puddings

Gaspé Oyster and Apple Soup

Rich but still light-bodied, this classic soup should be served in small cups so that it doesn't spoil appetites for the splendid dishes that follow.

2 tbsp (30 mL)	butter
1	small onion, finely chopped
1	small apple, peeled, cored and finely chopped
1/2 cup (125 mL)	finely chopped celery
1/2 tsp (2 mL)	salt
1/4 tsp (1 mL)	each nutmeg, cayenne and dry mustard
1	bay leaf
1/2 cup (125 mL)	Calvados, pommeaux or dry apple cider
2 cups (500 mL)	fresh or frozen and thawed shucked oysters and their juices
1 1/2 cups (375 mL)	each milk and 35% whipping cream
	Apple slices

Melt butter in a large saucepan or Dutch oven set over medium heat. Add onion, apple, celery, salt, nutmeg, cayenne, mustard and bay leaf. Cook, stirring often, for 5 minutes or until onion is softened. Add Calvados and stir for 1 minute or until evaporated.

Add oysters and their juices and poach just until the edges of the oysters begin to curl. Pour in milk and cream and heat until steaming. Do not boil. Taste and adjust seasoning if necessary. (Can be made ahead to this point, cooled, covered and refrigerated for up to 1 day. If making ahead, reheat without boiling.)

Ladle into soup cups and garnish with a slice of apple. Makes 6 servings.

Cider-raisin Glazed Pork Loin Roast

Anxious about carving a roast with expertise? Lay your fears aside; this mahogany showpiece is boneless, so it's very easy to carve. Thinly slice any leftovers and use them later in the week to make sandwiches slathered with honey mustard.

1 cup (250 mL)	apple cider or juice
1/4 cup (50 mL)	raisins
2 tbsp (30 mL)	chopped fresh thyme
2 tbsp (30 mL)	honey mustard
2	shallots or 1 small onion, chopped
2	cloves garlic
3 lb (1.5 kg)	tied, boneless double-loin pork roast
1 tsp (5 mL)	salt
1/2 tsp (2 mL)	pepper

Combine apple cider, raisins, thyme, mustard, shallots and garlic in a blender or mini-chopper. Blend until smooth. Place in a bowl or zip-top plastic bag. Add roast and turn to coat. Cover or seal and refrigerate for at least 4 hours or overnight.

Preheat oven to 425F (220C). Bring roast to room temperature for 30 minutes. Drain marinade into a small saucepan and bring to a boil. Reduce heat and simmer until thickened, 2 to 3 minutes; reserve. Set roast on a rack in a roasting pan and sprinkle all over with salt and pepper.

Roast, basting with reserved marinade at least twice, for 60 to 70 minutes or until an instant-read thermometer inserted into centre of meat registers 160F (71C). Let rest for 15 minutes before carving. Makes 6 servings.

Cauliflower and Oka Skillet Soufflé

Mild semi-soft Oka is one of Quebec's most famous cheeses, and it lends a wonderful full flavour to this rustic version of a soufflé. Don't worry if your soufflé doesn't roll perfectly. It will still taste sensational.

1 cup (250 mL)	milk
3 tbsp (45 mL)	butter
2 tbsp (30 mL)	all-purpose flour
1/4 tsp (1 mL)	each salt, pepper and nutmeg
4	eggs, separated
2 cups (500 mL)	small fresh cauliflower florets, cooked
1 cup (250 mL)	shredded Oka cheese

Topping:

2 tbsp (30 mL)	shredded Oka cheese

Preheat oven to 350F (180C). Heat milk in a saucepan or microwaveable dish until steaming. Melt 2 tbsp (30 mL) of the butter in a large saucepan set over medium heat. Sprinkle flour over butter and stir until blended. Cook, stirring, over medium heat until bubbly but not brown.

Whisk in a little milk until flour mixture is smooth. Add remaining milk; cook, whisking, for 2 to 3 minutes or until thickened and smooth. Remove from heat and stir in salt, pepper and nutmeg. Beat egg yolks and stir into sauce. Stir in cauliflower and 1 cup (250 mL) cheese. Using clean beaters, beat egg whites until stiff peaks form. Fold into cauliflower mixture with a rubber spatula.

Brush the inside of a 10-inch (25 cm) or 12-inch (30 cm) cast-iron or other heavy skillet with remaining butter. Turn batter into pan, smoothing with spatula to fill pan evenly. (Can be made ahead to this point, covered and refrigerated for up to 2 hours.)

Set pan over medium heat. Cook for 3 to 5 minutes or until puffed and golden on the bottom. Transfer to preheated oven and cook for 10 to 15 minutes or until lightly golden on top.

Loosen sides and bottom of soufflé with a flexible metal spatula. Use spatula to fold sides into centre, omelette-style. Turn out onto a platter and sprinkle top with 2 tbsp (30 mL) cheese. Serve at once. Makes 6 servings.

Brussels Sprout Leaves in Whisky-orange Sauce

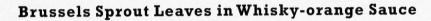

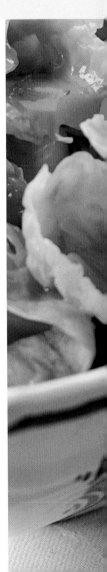

Because the leaves of brussels sprouts cook so much faster than whole heads, their flavour doesn't become too strong, and it's further enhanced by the addition of Quebec maple syrup and Canadian whisky.

8 cups (2 L)	brussels sprouts (about 1 1/4 lb/625 g)
1 tbsp (15 mL)	butter
1 tbsp (15 mL)	maple syrup
2 tbsp (30 mL)	Canadian whisky
1 tsp (5 mL)	finely grated orange peel
	Salt and pepper

Cut stem ends from brussels sprouts and separate heads into individual leaves. Boil in a pot of boiling salted water for 3 to 4 minutes or until almost tender. Drain well. (Can be made ahead to this point, refreshed under cold water, drained and reserved in refrigerator for up to 1 day.)

Heat butter in a skillet set over medium-high heat. Add maple syrup and whisky and bring to a boil. Add reserved brussels sprout leaves. Toss to coat. Stir in orange peel and salt and pepper to taste. Cook until leaves are tender. Makes 6 to 8 servings.

Blueberry White-chocolate Puddings

These homey puddings are similar to old-fashioned Quebec desserts, except that they've been updated with a trendy white-chocolate sauce. Some of the best blueberries in the country are grown in Quebec. Use the small wild ones if you can find them; otherwise, substitute the larger cultivated variety.

2 cups (500 mL)	fresh or frozen blueberries, thawed and drained
1 tsp (5 mL)	finely grated lemon peel
6 oz (175 g)	coarsely chopped white chocolate
2 cups (500 mL)	all-purpose flour
1 tsp (5 mL)	baking powder
1/4 tsp (1 mL)	salt
1/2 cup (125 mL)	butter, softened
1 cup (250 mL)	granulated sugar
2	eggs
1 tsp (5 mL)	vanilla
1 cup (250 mL)	milk
1/2 cup (125 mL)	35% whipping cream

Preheat oven to 350F (180C). Toss blueberries with lemon peel and 1/4 cup (50 mL) of the chocolate; reserve. Stir together flour, baking powder and salt; reserve. In a large bowl, beat butter until creamy and smooth. Add sugar and beat until fluffy. Add eggs, beating, one at a time. Stir in vanilla. Add flour mixture and milk alternately in two additions each to the butter mixture, beating well after each addition. Fold in blueberry mixture.

Tip: For flawless removal from ramekins, line bottom of each one with a small piece of waxed or parchment paper.

Spoon batter into prepared ramekins. Place in a baking or roasting pan and pour in enough boiling water to come halfway up sides of ramekins. Cover with foil and make a few vent holes. Bake for 35 to 40 minutes or until a tester inserted in the centre comes out clean. Cool for 10 to 15 minutes in a small saucepan or microwaveable dish.

Combine remaining white chocolate with whipping cream. Bring to a boil and stir until smooth. Run a knife around the edge of each pudding and turn out onto a serving dish. Drizzle with white-chocolate sauce. Makes 8 servings.

What to Serve With La Belle Cuisine

The words "warm" and "rich" describe the aromas and flavours in this menu, so it calls for wines that are full and distinct enough to enhance the fall flavours. For a crisp contrast to the slightly sweet, creamy, savoury character of the Gaspé Oyster and Apple Soup, try a Californian Fumé Blanc; many are medium body with hints of herb and spicy oak.

The Pork Loin Roast and the Cauliflower and Oka Skillet Soufflé have full, rich, tangy, slightly sweet and savoury flavours. The interesting orange and whisky accents in the Brussels Sprout Leaves also need a fuller-flavoured accompaniment. Riesling will work well with all these dishes. There is just enough body, sweetness and fruity citrus flavour here to enhance as well as cut through the full, sweetish richness.

The white-chocolate citrus-accented blueberry dessert needs no wine to lift its delicate flavours. But you can finish up with a well-blended mild coffee complemented with a splash of Grand Marnier.

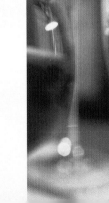

Shoestring Entertaining

Want to entertain like a sultan but stay within a budget? This make-ahead menu combines exotic flavours to create a lavish spread that no one will suspect costs less per person to serve than movie admission. Plus, this menu delivers generous amounts of fibre and is relatively light, so your wallet will be the only heavy thing you'll lug around after the party.

MENU

Red-pepper Hummus With Pita Triangles
and Black Olives

Spice-tent Roasted Chicken

Eggplant and Zucchini Fricassee

10-minute Couscous

Only-apples Flan With Crème Anglaise

Red-pepper Hummus With Pita Triangles and Black Olives

This easy-to-prepare starter makes a nice change from the ubiquitous cheese and crackers, and it doesn't take much more time to prepare. Save any leftover hummus to use as a spread for sandwiches later in the week.

1	red pepper
1	can (19 oz/540 mL) cooked chickpeas
2 tbsp (30 mL)	extra-virgin olive oil
1 tbsp (15 mL)	lightly packed mint leaves
1 tbsp (15 mL)	lemon juice
2	cloves garlic, minced
1/2 tsp (2 mL)	ground cumin
1/2 tsp (2 mL)	each salt and pepper
3	pita breads
1/2 cup (125 mL)	black olives

Preheat oven to 375F (190C). Place red pepper on a lightly oiled baking pan and place in oven. Roast, turning occasionally, for 30 to 40 minutes or until softened and browned in places. Remove from oven and cover tightly. Cool to room temperature. Peel away skin and discard. Cut pepper in half and remove white membranes, seeds and stem; discard.

Drain and rinse chickpeas. Place in a blender with red pepper, olive oil, mint leaves, lemon juice, garlic, cumin, salt and pepper. Blend until smooth. Taste and adjust seasoning if necessary. (Can be made ahead to this point, covered and refrigerated for up to 1 day. Taste and adjust seasoning before serving.)

Toast pitas and cut into small triangles. Serve hummus in a small bowl surrounded by pita triangles with olives on the side. Makes 6 servings.

Spice-tent Roasted Chicken

The beauty of this chicken is that it is as delicious at room temperature as it is hot, so if you'd rather socialize than cook while the hummus is passed, you can. Although this recipe uses a few exotic spices, you don't have to purchase pricey large-sized bottles if you go to a bulk store, where you can buy just the amounts you need.

1	small onion, grated
1/4 cup (50 mL)	orange juice
2 tbsp (30 mL)	brown sugar
1/2 tsp (2 mL)	finely grated lime peel
1 tbsp (15 mL)	lime juice
1	large clove garlic, minced
1 tbsp (15 mL)	finely grated gingerroot
1 tsp (5 mL)	each cinnamon and dried oregano
1/2 tsp (2 mL)	ground coriander seeds
1/4 tsp (1 mL)	ground cardamom
1/4 tsp (1 mL)	each salt and pepper
2	whole roasting chickens (about 4 lb/2 kg each)

Stir together onion, orange juice, brown sugar, lime peel, juice, garlic, ginger, cinnamon, oregano, coriander, cardamom, salt and pepper.

Rinse chickens inside and out, removing giblets and neck if in the cavities. Pat dry. Place chickens in a large bowl or in zip-top bags. Pour in orange-juice mixture, turning chickens to coat all over. Cover tightly and let marinate for at least 4 hours or up to 2 days.

Preheat oven to 375F (190C). Bring chickens to room temperature for 30 minutes, then place on a rack set over a roasting pan. Roast in the oven for about 1 1/2 hours or until an instant-read thermometer inserted into the body near the inner thigh reads 180F (82C). Let rest for 10 minutes before carving. Remove skin (optional). Makes 6 to 8 servings.

Eggplant and Zucchini Fricassee

Don't worry about adding the extra salt necessary to extract the bitter juices from the eggplant. It's removed before you start cooking and won't have a great effect on the sodium content of this make-ahead side dish. This mélange of vegetables is sensational served in a pita bread slathered with Red-pepper Hummus, so you may want to save a little of each for your lunch box.

1 tbsp (15 mL)	salt
2	large eggplants, thickly sliced
2	zucchini
3 tbsp (45 mL)	olive oil
2	onions, peeled and thinly sliced
3/4 tsp (4 mL)	ground cumin
1/2 tsp (2 mL)	paprika
1/4 tsp (1 mL)	yellow mustard seeds
1 cup (250 mL)	canned diced tomatoes
2 tbsp (30 mL)	balsamic vinegar
1 tsp (5 mL)	finely grated lemon peel
2 tbsp (30 mL)	each chopped coriander leaves and mint or basil
1/4 tsp (1 mL)	each salt and pepper

Sprinkle salt lightly over eggplant and set in a colander for 20 minutes. Discard bitter juices that drain from eggplant. Rinse and pat eggplant dry with paper towel. Coarsely chop eggplant and zucchini and reserve.

Heat oil in a Dutch oven set over medium heat. Add onions, cumin, paprika and mustard seeds. Cook for 7 minutes. Add eggplant and zucchini and cook, stirring often, for 5 minutes or until lightly browned. Stir in tomatoes and vinegar.

Reduce heat and simmer, stirring occasionally, for 10 to 12 minutes or until eggplant is very tender. Stir in lemon peel, coriander and mint. Season with salt and pepper, adding more to taste. Serve hot or at room temperature. Makes 8 servings.

10-minute Couscous

Couscous is a tiny pasta made by rubbing raw pasta dough over a coarse strainer. The instant variety is supremely easy to prepare, and because it expands many times in size when rehydrated, it is good value per package. The fennel seeds add a mild licorice note to this side dish, which adds complexity and depth to the overall menu.

2 cups (500 mL)	vegetable or chicken broth
2 cups (500 mL)	tomato juice
2 cups (500 mL)	instant couscous
1/2 tsp (2 mL)	each paprika and fennel seeds
1/4 tsp (1 mL)	ground pepper
Pinch	salt
1/2 cup (125 mL)	chopped green onions
1 cup (250 mL)	finely chopped fresh parsley
	Lemon wedges

Bring broth and tomato juice to a boil. Place couscous, paprika, fennel seeds, pepper and salt in a large bowl. Pour boiling broth over them and cover tightly. Let stand for 5 minutes. Fluff gently with a fork.

Stir in green onions and parsley. Taste and adjust seasoning if necessary. Serve with lemon wedges. Makes 6 servings.

Only-apples Flan With Crème Anglaise

This cunning apple dessert truly highlights the natural appeal of apples and has all the appeal of a cake but far fewer carbohydrates. Crème anglaise is a classic custard-style sauce that goes with almost any dessert.

12	Northern Spy or Spartan apples (about 3 ½ lb/1.6 kg)
½ cup (125 mL)	granulated sugar
2 tbsp (30 mL)	melted butter
1 tsp (5 mL)	each ground cinnamon and finely grated lemon peel
½ cup (125 mL)	dried cranberries

Crème Anglaise:

6	egg yolks
¼ cup (50 mL)	granulated sugar
Pinch	salt
2 cups (500 mL)	hot homogenized milk
1 tbsp (15 mL)	brandy
1 tsp (5 mL)	vanilla extract

Peel and core apples. Slice thinly into rings and toss with sugar, butter, cinnamon and lemon peel until well combined. Toss with cranberries. Preheat oven to 250F (120C). Arrange fruit mixture evenly in an 8-inch (2 L) springform pan.

Place pan on a rimmed baking sheet. Bake in preheated oven for 3 hours or until apples are very tender. Cool to room temperature. Spoon some crème anglaise on each of 8 serving plates. Place a wedge of apple flan on top and serve. Makes 8 servings.

Crème Anglaise:

Beat egg yolks with sugar and salt on medium speed for 3 to 4 minutes or until thick and light. Stir in milk. Transfer to a saucepan. Place pan over medium heat and cook, stirring gently, until custard is thick enough that a line forms when you draw your fingertip across the back of the spoon. Strain custard and stir in brandy and vanilla. Cool to room temperature and store, tightly covered, in refrigerator. Makes 2 1/2 cups (625 mL).

Tip: If you don't have time to make the crème anglaise, melt some premium vanilla ice cream and drizzle that on the dessert plates instead. The taste will be quite similar, since the base for ice cream is much like this sauce.

What to Serve With Shoestring Entertaining

This feast requires versatile wines to match the wonderful array of spices from cumin to fennel and cardamom. The ideal wine matches for full-flavoured spicier foods are those with good fruit flavours and perhaps a hint of sweetness. You won't have to break the budget for these good-value wines with great flavour.

The Red-pepper Hummus calls for a light white wine with lively acidity, such as a dry Riesling, which will balance the creaminess of the spread.

A flavourful dish such as Spice-tent Roasted Chicken, when matched with the vegetal flavours of eggplant and zucchini and the tomato couscous, requires a wine with good body and fruit flavours. However, the wine should not compete with these complex flavours but rather provide a wonderful backdrop. Chilean Sauvignon Blancs often have delicate melon flavours and refreshing acidity. If red wine is what you are looking for, a medium-bodied Montepulciano d'Abruzzo is a great and economical match, with its red berry flavours and balancing acidity.

The perfect fall dessert with apples and crème anglaise calls for a sweeter dessert wine such as spiced apple wine or Late Harvest Vidal. Both offer good value, and they are sure to please.

WINTER

Canadian winters offer many wonderful reasons to cook for your family and friends: the holidays, ski-chalet weekends, games nights, skating parties, Valentine's Day and plain old cabin fever are all great reasons to send out a call to your group that dinner is to be served at your place. And if the party happens at home, you can avoid having to bundle up and face the elements yourself!

This chapter showcases menus that feature recipes for stick-to-your-ribs foods. Besides being comforting, many of these menus are elegant enough to serve proudly at swish affairs. For time-crunched events, there are quick sautés such as Trout Almondine, and for potlucks, there are make-ahead entrées such as Two-cheese Baked Penne With Roasted Vegetables. All of these menus have been streamlined wherever possible so that almost every dish can be managed even if you feel swamped by the holidays or downcast about long transit delays due to snowy weather. Who could ask for better news? After all, one of the best ways to beat the winter blues is to have something good to eat!

One of the keys to entertaining successfully during the winter is to make your home a cosy sanctuary. If you don't have a fireplace, then candles, candles and more candles are in order. Likewise, close the drapes against the chill and add cushions to your dining chairs so that your guests feel enveloped in warmth and comfort the moment they come to the table.

You may even want to pass around warm towels before dinner is served. They are easy to prepare. Just moisten as many matching facecloths as you have guests with a mild solution of water and either lemon juice or rosewater. Wring out the cloths until just damp. Roll into cigar shapes and place them in a shallow casserole dish in a single layer; cover with plastic wrap. Just before you call everyone to the table, pop the container into the microwave for 40 or 50 seconds. Pass a steamy towel to each person at the table using tongs, but be sure to warn everyone that the towels are hot before they grab them.

Candlelit Christmas Eve Dinner

The family portion of holiday celebrations often begins for many Canadians on Christmas Eve. Since last-minute shopping, readying the house for guests and decorating for "the big day" also happen then, dinner needs to be special but easy to prepare. This festive menu fills the bill, combining holiday colours and seasonal flavours in a meal that is light enough not to ruin appetites for the big feast to come.

MENU

Martin's Lemon-parsnip Soup

Wilted Spinach Salad

Trout Almondine

Leek, Mushroom and Wild and White Rice Pilaf

Caramelized Pear-cranberry Strudel

Martin's Lemon-parsnip Soup

This cream-free purée is adapted from a recipe in Toronto chef Martin Kouprie's repertoire for Pangaea Restaurant. It makes a warming starter and is ideal served with crusty rolls or rustic bread sticks.

1 tbsp (15 mL)	butter or vegetable oil
1	onion, peeled and chopped
2 tbsp (30 mL)	chopped fresh thyme
1 tsp (5 mL)	finely grated lemon peel
1/2 tsp (2 mL)	salt
1/2 tsp (2 mL)	pepper
6 cups (1.5 L)	peeled, chopped parsnips
10 cups (2.5 L)	chicken or vegetable broth
1 tbsp (15 mL)	lemon juice
	Thyme sprigs
	Lemon slices

Heat butter in a large saucepan set over medium heat. Add the onion, thyme, lemon peel, salt and pepper. Cook, stirring often, for 5 minutes. Add the parsnips; cover and reduce heat to medium-low.

Simmer, stirring occasionally, for 10 minutes or until parsnips are tender. Stir in broth and bring to a boil. Cook, stirring, for 20 to 25 minutes or until parsnips are very soft. Transfer parsnip mixture to a blender or food processor in batches.

Purée until smooth. Stir in lemon juice and bring to a boil. Taste and adjust seasoning if necessary. Serve in soup cups garnished with thyme and lemon. Makes 8 servings.

Wilted Spinach Salad

Featuring festive colours and a fresh, bracing edge, this salad is special without being fussy to prepare.

3	bacon strips
2	shallots or 1/4 cup (50 mL) finely chopped onion
1/4 cup (50 mL)	olive oil
2 tbsp (30 mL)	sherry vinegar
1/2 tsp (2 mL)	Dijon mustard
1 tsp (5 mL)	red peppercorns, lightly crushed
1/2 tsp (2 mL)	dried dillweed
1/4 tsp (1 mL)	granulated sugar
12 cups (3 L)	baby spinach leaves
2	red peppers, thinly sliced
1 cup (250 mL)	croutons

Slice bacon crosswise into 1/4-inch (5 mm) strips. Heat a deep skillet over medium-high heat. Add the bacon; cook, stirring often, until it begins to brown, from 2 to 3 minutes. Finely chop shallots and add to bacon. Reduce heat to medium and cook until shallots are softened and bacon is crisp.

Pour off as much excess fat as possible. Whisk oil with vinegar, mustard, peppercorns, dill and sugar. Pour into hot pan. Immediately add spinach. Remove from heat and toss for 45 seconds or until leaves are wilted.

Transfer to a shallow serving bowl. Add peppers and croutons and toss to combine. Taste and adjust seasoning if necessary. Makes 8 servings.

Trout Almondine

Although this elegant entrée comes from the classic realm of French chefs, it is easy and fast to prepare.

¹/₄ cup (50 mL)	butter
²/₃ cup (150 mL)	sliced almonds
¹/₄ cup (50 mL)	thinly sliced green onions
3 lb (1.5 kg)	trout, salmon-trout or arctic-char fillets
¹/₂ tsp (2 mL)	each salt and pepper
3 tbsp (45 mL)	lemon or lime juice
	Lemon wedges

Melt butter in a large nonstick skillet set over medium-high heat. Cook until butter no longer sizzles and is browned. Stir in almonds and green onions. Cook, stirring, for 1 minute or until golden. Remove nuts and onions from butter using a slotted spoon; reserve.

Sprinkle fish evenly with salt and pepper. Place fillets, skin side up, in hot pan. Cook for 5 minutes or until edges start to curl and bottom is golden. Turn and cook for 3 to 4 minutes or until fish flakes easily. Repeat until all fillets are cooked. Sprinkle with lemon juice.

Arrange on a serving platter. Return almonds and green onions to pan. Reheat, stirring, for 30 seconds. Pour pan juices, almonds and green onions evenly over fish. Serve with lemon wedges. Makes 8 servings.

Leek, Mushroom and Wild and White Rice Pilaf

Pressed for time? Make this woodsy side dish ahead of time and reheat it in the microwave just before serving.

2 cups (500 mL)	blended long-grain and wild rice
4 cups (1 L)	water
1	bay leaf
Pinch	salt
1 tbsp (15 mL)	vegetable oil (approx)
2	leeks (white part only), thinly sliced
2 tsp (10 mL)	finely chopped fresh rosemary leaves
1	clove garlic, minced
³/₄ tsp (4 mL)	each salt and pepper
2 cups (500 mL)	thinly sliced shiitake mushrooms, stems removed
2 tbsp (30 mL)	balsamic vinegar
1 cup (250 mL)	finely diced seeded tomatoes

Place rice in a deep saucepan. Add water, bay leaf and salt. Bring to a boil over medium-high heat. Reduce heat to low. Cover and simmer for 20 minutes. Remove from heat and scatter rice over a tray to cool. Discard bay leaf.

Heat oil in a deep nonstick skillet set over medium heat. Add leeks, rosemary, garlic, salt and pepper. Cook, stirring often, for 5 minutes. Increase heat to medium-high and add mushrooms. Cook, stirring often, for 5 minutes or until golden. Add extra oil if necessary.

Stir in vinegar and tomatoes. Cook for 1 minute or until moisture has evaporated. Stir in rice and toss to combine. Cook over medium heat, stirring, for 5 minutes or until rice is tender. Taste and adjust seasoning if necessary. Makes 8 servings.

Caramelized Pear-cranberry Strudel

Easy and stylish, this not-too-sweet dessert can be served warm or at room temperature. Offer guests their choice of vanilla ice cream or a slice of blue cheese as a garnish. Both go wonderfully well with the flavours in this strudel.

1/2 cup (125 mL)	each fresh and dried cranberries
1 tbsp (15 mL)	cornstarch
3	large ripe pears
1/2 cup (125 mL)	butter
1 cup (250 mL)	granulated white sugar
1 tsp (5 mL)	finely grated orange peel
1 tsp (5 mL)	ground ginger
1/2 tsp (2 mL)	ground cinnamon
6	sheets phyllo pastry
	Icing sugar

Toss fresh cranberries with cornstarch; reserve. Peel pears; core and chop into bite-size pieces. Melt 2 tbsp (30 mL) of the butter in a heavy skillet set over high heat. Add pears and toss to coat. Sprinkle with sugar and add fresh cranberries.

Cook, tossing, for about 5 minutes or until pears are golden and cranberries are beginning to split. Stir in dried cranberries, orange peel, ginger and cinnamon. Cool to room temperature.

Melt remaining butter. Spread a sheet of phyllo on counter and brush evenly with butter. Add remaining layers, brushing liberally with butter between each layer. Leaving a 1-inch (2.5 cm) border along one of the short sides of the pastry and at the top and bottom, spoon the pear mixture in a band down the side of the phyllo. Fold over the edge and roll to encase fruit.

Brush all edges with additional butter and press together to fully encase fruit. Place phyllo bundle, seam side down, on a foil-lined rimmed baking sheet. Brush remaining butter over top. (Can be made ahead to this point, covered and refrigerated for up to 1 day. Bring to room temperature for 30 minutes before baking.)

Preheat oven to 400F (200C). Slice three vent holes in strudel using a sharp knife. Bake for 20 minutes or until golden. Cool pan on a rack. Sprinkle with icing sugar. Slice and serve warm or at room temperature. Makes 8 servings.

What to Serve With
Candlelit Christmas Eve Dinner

To complement this Christmas Eve menu, choose wines that exhibit lively, crisp fruit without heavy oak or tannin to compete with the more delicate flavours of this meal. The delicate, lightly sweet, herb-edged parsnip flavours of the soup call for a style of wine with good body and lemony acidity, such as a Riesling or a Sauvignon Blanc. Both wines can also follow through to the spinach salad with its more herbal flavours.

Because the main-course dishes have some nutty, slightly sweet flavours as well as pleasant earthy notes in common, they are well matched with a crisp, fruity red wine such as Pinot Noir, with typical mushroom undertones that will make the shiitake mushrooms in the pilaf sing. If you prefer a white wine, try an unoaked Chardonnay, since you'll need crisp lemony body to cut the richness of these dishes.

Caramelized Pear-cranberry Strudel is a rich and tangy dessert. With or without ice cream on the side, the best accompaniment is a good cup of quality medium-blend coffee with a splash of Triple Sec. Its distinctive orange-citrus flavour is a perfect finish to this Christmas Eve repast.

Crowd-Pleasing Buffet

So often when family and friends gather for a meal, it
is a challenge to serve foods that all your guests will
enjoy. This menu has something for everyone, which
makes it a surefire crowd-pleaser.
The full-flavoured vegetarian pasta dish
is a lot more interesting and easier to make
than old standbys such as lasagna.
And this hearty main course is
balanced with lighter appetizers,
a colourful salad and a decadent dessert.

MENU

Antipasto Platter With Crusty
Baguettes

Two-cheese Baked Penne With
Roasted Vegetables

Green and Red Salad

Winter Fruit-salad Bowl With Marsala

Ginger Brownies

Two-cheese Baked Penne With Roasted Vegetables

This full-flavoured pasta dish can be made ahead, so it's appropriate for weeknight entertaining as well as for taking to potluck dinners.

2	sweet red or yellow peppers, sliced
1/2 lb (250 g)	mushrooms, halved or quartered
2	small zucchini, sliced
2	small red onions, cut into chunks
4	cloves garlic, minced
1/4 cup (50 mL)	olive oil
	Salt and pepper
2 tbsp (30 mL)	chopped fresh basil or 2 tsp (10 mL) dried
1/2 tsp (2 mL)	dried rosemary
1/2 cup (125 mL)	chopped fresh parsley
1 lb (500 g)	penne pasta with ridges, cooked
3 1/2 cups (875 mL)	meatless spaghetti sauce (or one large can or jar plus tomato sauce to make 3 1/2 cups/875 mL)
1 lb (500 g)	provolone or mozzarella cheese, shredded
1 cup (250 mL)	freshly grated Asiago or Parmesan cheese

Preheat oven to 450F (230C). Toss peppers, mushrooms, zucchini, onions and garlic with oil. Roast in a large shallow pan for about 25 minutes or until softened, stirring once or twice. Season to taste with salt and pepper and stir in basil, rosemary and 1/3 cup (75 mL) of the parsley. Reduce oven temperature to 375F (190C).

Combine pasta, sauce, vegetables, provolone and half the Asiago. Transfer to a greased 13- x 9-inch (3 L) baking dish. Sprinkle with remaining Asiago and parsley. (Can be covered and refrigerated for up to 1 day or frozen for up to 2 months; thaw frozen casserole in refrigerator. Bring to room temperature before heating.)

Bake, covered, in preheated oven for 30 minutes. Uncover and bake for about 10 minutes longer or until hot throughout. Makes 8 servings.

Green and Red Salad

This crisp, colourful salad makes a nice foil for the rich casserole.

Dressing:

2	cloves garlic, minced
1 tbsp (15 mL)	each balsamic and white-wine vinegar
1 tsp (5 mL)	crumbled dried rosemary
1/2 tsp (2 mL)	salt
1/4 tsp (1 mL)	pepper
1/3 cup (75 mL)	olive oil

Salad:

10 cups (2.5 L)	torn romaine lettuce
2 cups (500 mL)	torn radicchio
2 cups (500 mL)	packed Italian parsley leaves
1	small fennel bulb, trimmed and thinly sliced
1	small red onion, thinly sliced

Dressing:
Combine garlic, vinegars, rosemary, salt and pepper in a small jar. Gradually whisk in oil. (Can be made a day ahead, covered and refrigerated; before serving, bring to room temperature and shake well.)

Salad:
Place romaine and radicchio in a large salad bowl. Add parsley, fennel and onion. (Can be covered with a damp tea towel and refrigerated for up to 2 hours.) To serve, add dressing and toss well to coat. Makes 8 servings.

Antipasto Platter With Crusty Baguettes

An enticing array of Italian appetizers piques the appetite and stimulates con-
versation as guests help themselves. When you're short of time, you'll find a
good antipasto selection at most supermarkets and in Italian-food shops; add
home-made varieties as desired.

   If your guest list includes vegetarians, it might be wise to serve this on two
smaller plates, one that features meat and seafood and one with meat-free
components. Choose two or three kinds of olives, marinated artichoke hearts,
pickled mushrooms, pickled eggplant, roasted red-pepper strips, marinated
vegetables and marinated seafood. If desired, add Italian cheese, salami and
thinly sliced prosciutto to wrap around fresh fig quarters or melon slices.
Garnish with large leaves of fresh basil and clusters of small tomatoes. Set out
sliced crusty baguettes and individual plates.

Winter Fruit-salad Bowl With Marsala

Blending dried and fresh fruits in a compote makes for a very satisfying eating experience. Choose dried fruits that are soft and pliable for the best results. Minus the alcohol, this blend of fruits is also sensational and healthy for breakfast.

1 cup (250 mL)	dried figs
1 cup (250 mL)	dried apricots
1 1/2 cups (375 mL)	sweet Marsala wine
1/2 cup (125 mL)	water (approx)
2	large oranges
2	tangerines
3	pears
2 cups (500 mL)	small seedless red grapes
	Orange juice (optional)

Snip stems from figs; cut figs in half. Combine with apricots, Marsala and water in a small stainless steel saucepan. Cover and let soak (macerate) for 1 to 2 hours at room temperature or overnight in refrigerator. (If necessary after macerating, add a little more water before cooking; the fruit should be well covered with liquid.) Bring fig mixture to a boil; reduce heat, cover and simmer for 10 minutes or until fruit is very tender. Let cool.

Peel oranges and tangerines, paring off outer membrane. Holding fruit over a large bowl, cut away sections from between inner membranes. Squeeze any juice into bowl before discarding membranes. Peel pears (if desired), remove cores and cut into bite-size chunks. Add to orange sections in bowl. Add grapes and dried-fruit mixture. If the salad needs more liquid, add some orange juice. (Can be covered and refrigerated for up to 4 hours before serving.) Makes 8 servings (recipe can be easily doubled).

Ginger Brownies

These decadent brownies with cream-cheese icing are ultra-fudgy and wonderfully special because of the crystallized ginger.

Brownies

1/4 cup (50 mL)	unsweetened cocoa powder
3 tbsp (45 mL)	boiling water
3/4 cup (175 mL)	packed brown sugar
1/3 cup (75 mL)	butter, melted
1	egg
1 tsp (5 mL)	vanilla
1/2 cup (125 mL)	all-purpose flour
2/3 cup (150 mL)	chopped candied ginger

Preheat oven to 300F (150C). Mix cocoa with boiling water; reserve. Beat sugar with butter in a large bowl. Stir in egg, cocoa mixture and vanilla until smooth. Stir in flour and ginger. Spread batter evenly in a greased 8-inch (2 L) square cake pan.

Bake in preheated oven for 20 to 25 minutes or until set; don't overbake. (The brownies are quite shallow and very moist.) While still slightly warm, spread with chocolate cream-cheese icing (recipe follows). Cool, cover and refrigerate. (Can be stored in refrigerator for 2 to 3 days.) To serve, cut into small bars. Makes 24 bars.

Chocolate Cream-cheese Icing:

4 oz (125 g)	light cream cheese, softened
3 tbsp (45 mL)	light sour cream
1/2 cup (125 mL)	icing sugar
2 tbsp (30 mL)	unsweetened cocoa powder

Beat cream cheese with sour cream until very smooth. Sift icing sugar with cocoa and beat into cheese mixture until smooth.

What to Serve With Crowd-Pleasing Buffet

A buffet is very informal way of dining, where people serve themselves to food and also wines. Present a couple of choices so that the guests can experiment with different wine and food matches. Offer lighter-styled white wines to start, medium-bodied reds to match the main courses and a sweet wine to end the meal.

Italian whites, especially Arneis or those from Piedmont, are known for their delicacy and freshness and would work well with the antipasto platter. They both have enough flavour to complement the array of vegetables and not be too overwhelmed by the pickling.

Cabernet Franc wines are a good match for the vegetable pasta dish. This grape makes a wine with good fruit and a hint of green pepper and tobacco. The better Loire Valley reds are made with Cabernet Franc. They come from the appellations of Chinon, Bourgueil and St-Nicholas de Bourgueil. Quality Cabernet Franc also is made in Ontario; with some out-standing values are to be had.

A dessert wine will be a special way to end the meal. A tawny port will reflect the flavours of the dried fruits in the salad wonderfully and still have enough body and flavour to complement the chocolate and ginger in the brownies.

Trattoria Supper

Italian trattorias are casual cafés. They are loved because they serve uncomplicated food that sticks to your ribs – perfect fare for home cooks looking for a winter menu! While our trattoria menu is designed to make four servings, many of the dishes can be scaled down by half to create a cosy Valentine's Day dinner for two or doubled to serve a gathering of eight.

MENU

Blood-orange and Fennel Salad

Spaghetti With Pancetta and Mushrooms

Veal Rollatini With Sage Pesto

Balsamic-glazed Peppers and Onions

Caramel-mochaccino Semifreddo

Blood-orange and Fennel Salad

Called *finocchio* in Italy, fennel bulb is a lovely-looking pale green vegetable with a subtle anise flavour. Both fennel and tangy blood oranges (so named because of their dark burgundy and orange variegated flesh) are perfect for starting a rich meal because they cleanse the palate and ready it for the heavier dishes to come.

3		blood or navel oranges
1		large fennel bulb
4 tsp (20 mL)		white-wine vinegar
4 tsp (20 mL)		finely chopped basil
1		clove garlic, minced
1/4 tsp (1 mL)		each salt and pepper
1/4 cup (50 mL)		extra-virgin olive oil

Use a sharp knife to remove peel from oranges. Cut oranges into segments, removing all the white pith. Slice end from fennel and remove shoots from top; reserve fennel tops. If exterior of bulb is marred or discoloured, peel with a vegetable peeler. Cut bulb in half and thinly slice.

Whisk vinegar with basil, garlic, salt and pepper. Whisk in oil. Arrange fennel slices and orange segments on serving dishes. Drizzle dressing over salads and garnish with reserved fennel fronds. Makes 4 servings.

Spaghetti With Pancetta and Mushrooms

While a pasta dish such as this one is often a weeknight entrée here in Canada, in this menu, it is served as the second course, before the main course. Needless to say, servings of this delicious pasta should be small so that your guests are able to enjoy the next two courses to come.

1/2 lb (250 g)	dry spaghetti
1/4 cup (50 mL)	extra-virgin olive oil
2 oz (60 g)	diced pancetta or bacon
2 cups (500 mL)	sliced mushrooms such as button, cremini and shiitake
2 tsp (10 mL)	capers
2	cloves garlic, minced
1/4 tsp (1 mL)	salt
1/8 tsp (0.5 mL)	hot pepper flakes
2 tbsp (30 mL)	chopped fresh parsley or basil
	Parmesan cheese

Cook spaghetti until al dente in a large pot of salted water. Drain well and reserve. Heat 1 tbsp (15 mL) of the olive oil in a skillet set over low heat. Add pancetta and mushrooms and cook, stirring, until browned.

Add remaining oil, capers, garlic, salt and hot pepper flakes. Cook, stirring, for about 10 minutes or until garlic is just slightly golden. Stir in parsley and toss with cooked noodles. Serve with Parmesan cheese on the side. Makes 4 servings.

Veal Rollatini With Sage Pesto

These elegant little bundles are wonderful for dinner parties, be they large or small. For a buffet, they can be stacked on a platter, or for a more formally served dinner party, they can be arranged nicely on serving plates.

Sage Pesto:

1/2 cup (125 mL)	each lightly packed fresh sage and parsley
2	cloves garlic
1/2 cup (125 mL)	grated Parmesan cheese
1 tbsp (15 mL)	lemon juice
3/4 tsp (4 mL)	salt
1/4 cup (50 mL)	extra-virgin olive oil

Rollatini:

8	slices veal or turkey scaloppine (about 1 lb/500 g)
1/4 tsp (1 mL)	pepper

Sage Pesto:

Combine sage and parsley in a mini-chopper or blender. Add garlic, cheese, lemon juice and 1/2 tsp (2 mL) salt. Pulse to combine. Add oil and blend until well mixed.

Rollatini:

Place meat on a clean work surface. Pat dry and sprinkle evenly with pepper and remaining salt. Spread pesto evenly over each piece of meat, leaving a finger-width border at the end. Roll up each piece tightly, starting at the shorter end, and securely close with a toothpick.

Heat a large greased skillet over medium-high heat. Add rolls and cook, turning often, for 3 to 5 minutes or until browned on all sides. Cover and cook for 3 minutes longer or until cooked through. Remove toothpicks before serving. Makes 4 servings.

Balsamic-glazed Peppers and Onions

This colourful, easy side dish can be converted into a pasta sauce or stir-fry for simple, elegant weeknight cooking.

2 tbsp (30 mL)	vegetable oil
1	onion, peeled and thinly sliced
1	clove garlic, minced
4 tsp (20 mL)	chopped fresh oregano
1/2 tsp (2 mL)	each salt and pepper
1	each red, yellow and green peppers, thinly sliced
2 tbsp (30 mL)	balsamic vinegar
1 tsp (5 mL)	liquid honey
1/2 tsp (2 mL)	minced gingerroot

Heat half the oil in a large wok or deep skillet set over medium-high heat. Add the onion and cook, partially covered, for 5 to 7 minutes, stirring occasionally. Add garlic, oregano, salt and pepper and cook for 3 minutes.

Add remaining oil to pan and stir in peppers. Cook, stirring often, for 5 minutes or until peppers are browned. Stir in vinegar, honey and ginger. Toss for about 1 minute or until peppers are well glazed. Makes 4 servings.

Caramel-mochaccino Semifreddo

Semifreddo – the Italian word for "half cold" – refers here to a creamy frozen dessert. Serve this rich, decadent treat with rolled wafer biscuits or some other very crisp cookie.

Caramel:

3/4 cup (175 mL)	granulated sugar
1/4 cup (50 mL)	water

Semifreddo:

4 oz (125 g)	bittersweet or semi-sweet chocolate, chopped
2 1/2 cups (625 mL)	35% whipping cream
1/2 cup (125 mL)	granulated sugar
6	egg yolks
1 tsp (5 mL)	instant coffee granules
1/4 cup (50 mL)	coffee-flavoured liqueur or strong coffee

Caramel:

Stir sugar with water in a small saucepan set over medium heat until sugar dissolves. Bring to a boil and cook, without stirring, for 10 to 12 minutes or until amber. (Brush sides of pan with water if crystals form.) Immediately pour onto a lightly buttered foil-lined rimmed baking sheet.

Semifreddo:

Place chocolate in a bowl. Heat 3/4 cup (175 mL) of the cream until steaming and pour over chocolate. Stir until smooth; reserve. Beat sugar with egg yolks and coffee granules in a small heatproof bowl. Set over barely simmering water and whisk for 3 to 5 minutes or until pale and fluffy. Stir in liqueur and cook, stirring constantly, for 6 to 8 minutes or until thickened. Cool to room temperature.

Whip remaining cream until very thick. Fold in egg mixture. Chop caramel into small pieces.

Line a 9- x 5-inch (2 L) loaf pan with waxed paper. Spread one-third of the egg mixture in bottom of pan. Drizzle with half the chocolate mixture and sprinkle with half the caramel. Repeat each layer, spreading gently. Top with remaining egg mixture and smooth evenly. Cover and place in freezer for at least 6 hours or up to 1 week. Remove from freezer 10 minutes before serving. Makes 10 servings.

What to Serve With Trattoria Supper

Blood-orange and Fennel Salad, with its tangy citrus, mild liquorice and light, sweet herbal character, calls for a combination of refreshing effervescence and acidity, which the delightfully fizzy Italian sparkling wine Prosecco can offer. This sparkler's hint of sweetness and light pear, anise and citrus-fruit flavours harmonize with those in the salad.

Our pasta course, Spaghetti With Pancetta and Mushrooms, has an appealing earthy, herbal edge that is well matched by a Pinot Noir, which exhibits distinctive earthy, spiced-cherry and dried-herb flavours. If white is your preference, choose a Chardonnay to contrast and complement the salty and creamy richness that the olive oil and pancetta impart.

The Veal Rollatini With Sage Pesto and the Balsamic-glazed Peppers and Onions provide very different but interesting flavour combinations. Two very different red wines will work well with either dish. Campofiorin from Italy, with ripe, rich cherry fruit and soft plumminess, provides a great contrast to the pungent flavours of Parmesan cheese and sage. Its fruitiness and rounded, velvety texture also provide a wonderful complement to the rich, sweet flavours of the peppers and onions. Or, to pick up on the herbal notes in both dishes, try a Cabernet-Merlot blend with dark berry and savoury fresh herbal hints to do the trick.

Light and airy, the Caramel-mochaccino Semifreddo dessert is ideal savoured with a cup of freshly brewed light-bodied coffee enhanced with a splash of coffee-flavoured liqueur.

Hong Kong Experience

Hong Kong, where some of the world's best chefs perform their magic in well over 30,000 restaurants offering every type of international cuisine and all of China's regional foods (including Shanghainese, Pekinese, Szechuan, Hunan and Cantonese) is a true food-lover's paradise.

Some say that Cantonese-style food is the true cuisine of Hong Kong because most Hong Kong residents originated from Guangdong province, where Canton is located. So take a trip to Hong Kong with this menu of Cantonese-style chinese dishes developed especially for Canadian home cooks.

MENU

Hot and Sour Soup

Szechuan Chicken and Peanuts With Chili Peppers

Six-colour Vegetable Platter

Steamed Shrimp With Hot Ginger Soy Sauce

Cantonese Barbecued Spareribs

Steamed White Rice (recipe not included)

Fresh Fruit Salad (recipe not included)

Hot and Sour Soup

The Cantonese think of soup not only as a delicious food but also as essential therapy for rehydrating the body and skin.

12 oz (375 g)	tofu (firm or extra-firm)
1 cup (250 mL)	Chinese dried mushrooms
8 cups (2 L)	chicken broth
1/2 lb (250 g)	lean pork butt, slivered
1 1/2 cups (375 mL)	matchstick-cut bamboo shoots (fresh or canned, rinsed)
2 tbsp (30 mL)	rice vinegar
1 tbsp (15 mL)	Worcestershire sauce or Chinese black vinegar
1 tbsp (15 mL)	rice wine or sherry
1 tbsp (15 mL)	minced gingerroot
1/2 tsp (2 mL)	each salt and pepper
2 tbsp (30 mL)	cornstarch
1 cup (250 mL)	frozen peas
1	egg, lightly beaten
2 tsp (10 mL)	sesame oil
1 tsp (5 mL)	chili oil (approx)
1	green onion, finely chopped

Cut tofu into thin julienne strips. In a small bowl, cover mushrooms with 3/4 cup (175 mL) warm water and let soak for 30 minutes. Drain and discard water. Trim off any tough stems and slice caps into thin julienne strips.

Bring chicken broth to a boil in a large pot. Add mushrooms, pork and bamboo shoots. Return to the boil, reduce heat, cover and simmer for 3 minutes. Add tofu, vinegar, Worcestershire sauce, rice wine, ginger, salt and pepper. (Can be prepared ahead to this point, cooled, covered and refrigerated.)

Heat to boiling if chilled, taste and adjust seasoning. Dissolve cornstarch in 1/4 cup (50 mL) cold water. Slowly whisk cornstarch mixture into hot soup, and simmer until thickened. Stir in peas and heat through.

Remove from heat and slowly add egg, pouring in a thin stream around edge and carefully stirring once or twice so that egg forms streamers. Transfer to heated tureen or serving bowl. Gently stir in sesame oil and chili oil. Sprinkle with green onion and serve immediately.
Makes 6 servings.

Serving a Traditional Chinese Meal

Typically, a Chinese meal for the family or for casual entertaining consists of about one different dish per person at the table. Everything is shared, and if more people come along, more dishes are added. Serve the soup first, then bring everything else (except dessert) to the table at the same time.

Szechuan Chicken and Peanuts With Chili Peppers

Szechuan vies with Hunan province for the spiciest of Chinese regional cuisines. This simple stir-fry is fiery-hot but still flavourful and well balanced.

2	whole chicken breasts
1 tbsp (15 mL)	minced gingerroot
2 tsp (10 mL)	light soy sauce
1/4 tsp (1 mL)	salt
1 tsp (5 mL)	cornstarch
2 tbsp (30 mL)	peanut or vegetable oil
1 cup (250 mL)	unsalted skinless peanuts
4	small dried red chili peppers
1 tsp (5 mL)	rice vinegar
1/2 tsp (2 mL)	granulated sugar
	Boston or leaf lettuce leaves

Cut chicken into 1/2-inch (1 cm) dice. In a bowl, combine chicken, ginger, soy sauce, salt and cornstarch.

Heat oil in a wok or skillet set over high heat, add peanuts and stir-fry for 2 minutes. Remove with slotted spoon and reserve. Add chili peppers and stir-fry for 1 minute. Remove with slotted spoon and reserve. Add chicken mixture and stir-fry for 2 minutes. Add vinegar, sugar, peanuts and chilies and heat through. Serve immediately on lettuce-lined platter. Makes 6 small servings.

Tip: Chinese chefs usually bone the chicken breasts but leave the skin on when dicing. You can do the same or use four boneless, skinless chicken breast halves.

Six-colour Vegetable Platter

Chinese home cooks make a couple of visits a day to the markets so that they have fresh ingredients for each meal. Although you might not want to do that, choose the freshest vegetables available.

1 tbsp (15 mL)	soy sauce
1 tsp (5 mL)	cornstarch
1/2 tsp (2 mL)	each salt and granulated sugar
2 tbsp (30 mL)	peanut or vegetable oil
1	clove garlic, minced
1	green onion, chopped
1 1/2 cups (375 mL)	small cauliflower florets
4	small carrots, thinly sliced diagonally
1/2 cup (125 mL)	vegetable or chicken broth
1	sweet red pepper, cut in strips
4 oz (125 g)	snow peas, trimmed
1	can (14 oz/398 mL) mini corn cobs, drained
1	can (14 oz/398 mL) straw mushrooms, drained

Stir together soy sauce, cornstarch, salt and sugar in a small bowl; reserve. Heat oil in wok over high heat. Add garlic and green onion and stir-fry for 10 seconds. Add cauliflower and carrots and stir-fry for 2 minutes. Pour half the broth around upper portion of wok and stir-fry for 1 minute. Add red pepper and snow peas and stir-fry for 2 minutes. Pour remaining broth around upper part of wok, add corn and mushrooms and stir-fry for 2 minutes.

Stir reserved cornstarch mixture into wok. Stir-fry until vegetables are coated. Arrange on platter and serve immediately. Makes 6 small servings.

Steamed Shrimp With Hot Ginger Soy Sauce

Fresh seafood abounds in Hong Kong, where many restaurants have tanks of live fish and seafood from which diners can choose their own meal.

1 1/2 lb (750 g)	medium shrimp in shells
2 tbsp (30 mL)	vegetable oil
1/3 cup (75 mL)	soy sauce
2 tbsp (30 mL)	shredded gingerroot
2	green onions, shredded
1	fresh red chili pepper, shredded

Wash shrimp well and place in ice water for 10 minutes. Transfer to a covered steamer set over boiling water. Cook for about 5 minutes or until just pink. Remove shells. Meanwhile, heat oil over high heat in a small saucepan. Stir in soy sauce, ginger, green onions and chili pepper. Arrange shrimp on hot platter. Pour sauce over top and serve immediately. Makes 6 small servings.

Cantonese Barbecued Spareribs

Chiu Chow cuisine originates in eastern Guangdong province. Guangzhou (Canton) is the local capital, and its food has a distinct character. These delicious oven-cooked ribs are easy to make and and very similar to the excellent ribs served in the inexpensive Chiu Chow restaurants of Hong Kong.

4 lb (2 kg)	lean pork spareribs
1/3 cup (75 mL)	hoisin sauce
1/4 cup (50 mL)	packed brown sugar
1 tbsp (15 mL)	rice wine or dry sherry
1 tbsp (15 mL)	oyster sauce
2	cloves garlic, crushed
1/2 tsp (2 mL)	five-spice powder
	Salt

Trim any fat from ribs and cut between bones into serving-size pieces. Place in a sturdy plastic bag or glass bowl. Stir together hoisin sauce, sugar, wine, oyster sauce, garlic and five-spice powder. Pour over ribs and rub to coat well. Cover and let marinate in refrigerator for at least 4 hours or up to 1 day.

Preheat oven to 400F (200C). Line a large, shallow roasting pan with foil and place a rack on top of foil. Arrange ribs, meaty side up, on rack. Roast in preheated oven for 10 minutes. Reduce heat to 375F (190C) and roast, turning occasionally and basting, for 1 to 1 1/4 hours or until tender. Sprinkle with salt to taste if needed. Makes 6 small servings.

What to Serve With Hong Kong Experience

This menu features both spicy and mild dishes with a variety of flavours. The wines should be fruity and off-dry to slightly sweet, so opt for an off-dry Riesling from Germany or Ontario. These make good matches and can be used throughout the meal if desired.

The shrimp and sparerib dishes require a fuller-bodied wine with great flavour. So an Alsatian Gewürztraminer with its lychee flavour will add an Asian flair to this meal. If a red wine is required, a wine from Gamay Noir would do well. This could be a Beaujolais or a Gamay from Ontario.

To finish a meal like this, do it in true Hong Kong style: bring out the icewine to put an exclamation point on this exotic menu.

Valentine's Day Dinner for Two

Rich, sumptuous and completely decadent, this
Valentine's Day dinner *pour deux* is truly over the top,
and it will surely impress your date.
Although the ingredients are unabashedly
luxurious, each recipe has been
developed to be prepared
in a home kitchen.

MENU

Artichokes With Chipotle Mayonnaise

Lobster-horseradish Mashed Potatoes

Seared Strip Loin With Foie-gras Sauce

Braised Baby Bok Choy With Lemon
and Lemon Grass

Molten-chocolate Indulgence Platter

Artichokes With Chipotle Mayonnaise

Nothing shows your appreciation for someone more than taking a little time to prepare a special vegetable like artichokes! If concerns about calories and fat are serious, add chipotle sauce to a low-fat mayonnaise instead of making our decadent home-made version.

2	whole lemons
1 tbsp (15 mL)	all-purpose flour
2	large globe artichokes

Mayonnaise:

4 tsp (20 mL)	lemon juice
1	egg yolk
1 tsp (5 mL)	Dijon mustard
1/2 tsp (2 mL)	each salt and white pepper
2/3 cup (150 mL)	canola or vegetable oil
1 1/2 tsp (7 mL)	spiced cayenne chipotle sauce

Cut 1 lemon in half; slice remaining lemon into quarters. Whisk flour into a large pot of salted water and stir in quartered lemons. Cover and bring to a boil. Cut the stem end from the base of each artichoke; peel off tough outer leaves and trim remaining leaves. Rub cut surface with lemon. Using a knife, trim around base of artichoke until rounded; rub well with lemon.

Immerse artichokes in boiling-water mixture; keep submerged by weighting down with a lid slightly smaller than the diameter of the pot. Simmer for about 25 minutes or until fork-tender; drain and immerse in cold water. Drain well and, using a teaspoon, scoop out and discard chokes. Place each artichoke on a plate and fan out leaves.

Mayonnaise:

Beat lemon juice, egg yolk, mustard, salt and pepper until thick using a stand-up mixer or a small food processor. Beating constantly, add half the oil, drop by drop, until very thick. Still beating, slowly drizzle in remaining oil; stir in chipotle sauce. Taste and adjust seasoning if necessary. Cover and reserve in refrigerator for up to 24 hours.

Spoon chipotle mayonnaise into the centre of each artichoke "flower" and serve. Makes 2 servings.

Lobster-horseradish Mashed Potatoes

While canned or frozen lobster can be used to prepare this side dish, it will be tastiest if you use a freshly steamed Atlantic lobster tail.

2	large potatoes (about 1 lb/500 g each), peeled and cut in chunks
2 tbsp (30 mL)	butter
1/4 cup (50 mL)	buttermilk or sour cream
3/4 tsp (4 mL)	horseradish
1/4 tsp (1 mL)	each salt and pepper
1/2 cup (125 mL)	cooked, chopped lobster meat

Cook potatoes, covered, for 20 minutes in a large pot of boiling salted water. Drain well and return pan to burner for 30 seconds or until bottom of pan is dry. Mash potatoes with a hand-held masher or a potato ricer until almost smooth, then return to pan.

Mix potatoes with butter, buttermilk, horseradish, salt and pepper. Whip by hand until fluffy using a wooden spoon. Fold in lobster. Taste and adjust seasoning if necessary. Makes 2 servings.

Seared Strip Loin With Foie-gras Sauce

Juicy steak paired with a decadent duck-liver sauce is well complemented by Lobster-horseradish Mashed Potatoes for a most upscale take on meat and potatoes.

1 oz (30 g)	each butter and fresh foie gras
1 lb (500 g)	strip loin steak
½ tsp (2 mL)	each salt and pepper
2 tsp (10 mL)	vegetable oil
1 tsp (5 mL)	balsamic vinegar
½ cup (125 mL)	beef or chicken broth, preferably home-made
1 tbsp (15 mL)	cognac

Blend butter with foie gras until smooth in a mini-chopper or using a fork. Scrape mixture onto a piece of waxed paper or plastic wrap. Shape into a disc and place in the freezer for 10 minutes or in refrigerator for 1 hour. Cut into small cubes and reserve in refrigerator.

Trim any excess fat from steak and sprinkle evenly with salt and pepper. Heat oil in a medium-sized heavy skillet over medium-high heat. Add steak and cook, turning once, for 14 minutes or until medium-rare. Drizzle balsamic vinegar over meat and turn steak to coat on both sides.

Remove steak from pan and tent loosely with foil. Add broth and cognac to pan. Bring to a boil. Reduce heat to low. Gradually whisk cubes of foie-gras mixture into sauce until thickened. Taste and adjust seasoning if necessary. Keep warm.

Slice meat on the diagonal into two equal portions. Pour a little sauce onto serving plates and top with steak. Serve additional sauce on the side. Makes 2 servings.

Tip: Fresh foie gras is available at specialty butchers and by special order at some grocery stores. It's pricey, so try to find a butcher who sells it in small quantities.

Braised Bok Choy With Lemon and Lemon Grass

Slightly astringent, this side dish is a good palate-cleanser when served next to a rich dish such as the Seared Strip Loin With Foie-gras Sauce.

¼ tsp (1 mL)	ground coriander seeds
2 cups (500 mL)	chicken or vegetable broth
1	lemon
1 tsp (5 mL)	chopped lemon grass (optional)
1	clove garlic, minced
¼ tsp (1 mL)	each salt and pepper
Pinch	hot chili flakes
2	small bok choy

Toast coriander for 1 minute or until fragrant (in saucepan set over medium heat). Stir in chicken broth. Using a zester or grater, remove yellow peel from lemon and add to broth. Halve lemon and squeeze juice into broth. Add lemon grass, garlic, salt, pepper and chili flakes. Bring to a boil.

Trim away root ends and any tattered or tough outer leaves on bok choy. Wash carefully under running water to remove grit trapped between leaves. Immerse in broth mixture and return to a boil.

Reduce heat and simmer, covered, for 7 to 10 minutes or until tender; remove from pot and serve immediately. Makes 2 servings.

Tip: Reserve cooking liquid to use as the base for a soup or sauce.

Molten-chocolate Indulgence Platter

Nothing is more traditional than chocolate on Valentine's Day. This style of dessert is ideal for nibbling slowly while you savour the moment with your lover on a romantic evening, but it's also a great answer any time you find yourself needing a fancy dessert in a hurry.

3 oz (90 g)	each bittersweet and milk chocolate
1/4 cup (50 mL)	35% whipping cream
2 tsp (10 mL)	cognac (optional)
	Whole strawberries, sliced banana, passion fruit and kiwi chunks (optional)
	Rolled wafer cookies (optional)

Chop chocolate into chunks and place in a heatproof dish. In a microwave-safe measuring cup, heat cream in microwave on high for 30 to 45 seconds or until steaming hot.

Pour over chocolate and stir until chocolate is melted. If necessary, heat chocolate mixture on medium for 30 seconds and stir until smooth. Stir in cognac, if using. Place dish on a platter and surround with a selection of fruit and cookies. Makes 2 servings.

What to Serve With Valentine's Day Dinner for Two

The zesty, mouth-watering flavours of Artichokes With Chipotle Mayonnaise call for a wine similar in style such as a dry Riesling with crisp citrus and mineral aromas and flavours.

With the Seared Strip Loin, try Pinot Noir, a dry red with berry fruit, spicy notes and good acidity. If you're a white-wine devotee, opt for a full-bodied Chardonnay with rich fruit flavours and toasty oak notes.

With the decadent Molten-chocolate Indulgence Platter, serve an icy bottle of Framboise, a sweet raspberry dessert wine that complements the chocolate. Another ideal match is icewine, which comes in 200-mL bottles, a perfect size for two.

Food and Love

Over time, the reputations of certain sensual-to-eat foods have become intertwined with romance. Whether the claim is that such foods will elicit passion or boost virility, aphrodisiac foods are usually special treats that go beyond most people's everyday repertoire.

While scientific verification of such claims is scant, just serving such fabled items may be hint enough to encourage a potential suitor. Here's a list of some foods commonly believed to be aphrodisiacs.

1. Artichokes
2. Asparagus
3. Avocado
4. Champagne
5. Chocolate
6. Figs
7. Grapes
8. Honey
9. Oysters
10. Rosemary

Ranch-Style Hospitality

Whether you're a rancher or an urban cowboy, western Canadian winters can b

bone-chilling. But when the weather's the coldest, the welcome's the warmest

So whether you're hosting a gathering of friends after a day on the ski slopes

or just braving winter in the city, here's a contemporary cowboy-style menu

that's sure to please.

MENU

Black-bean Nachos

Pork and Beef Chili With Ancho Sauce

Coleslaw With Old-fashioned Boiled
Dressing

Saskatoon-berry Potpie

Black-bean Nachos

Perfect for nibbling around the fire, these nachos are sure to please hungry friends who venture out into the cold to come to visit you.

Fresh Salsa:

2	plum tomatoes, seeded and chopped
1/4 cup (50 mL)	chopped onion
1 tbsp (15 mL)	freshly squeezed lime juice
1	jalapeño pepper, minced
2 tbsp (30 mL)	finely chopped coriander leaves
1 tbsp (15 mL)	finely chopped fresh parsley
1 tsp (5 mL)	each chopped fresh thyme and oregano (or 1/4 tsp/1 mL dried)
1	green onion, chopped

Refried Beans:

1 cup (250 mL)	cooked or canned black beans, drained and rinsed
1 tbsp (15 mL)	olive oil
1 tbsp (15 mL)	minced garlic
2	chili peppers (such as serrano or jalapeño), minced
1/4 cup (50 mL)	chopped coriander leaves
	Salt

Guacamole:

2	ripe avocados
3 tbsp (45 mL)	freshly squeezed lime juice
1 tsp (5 mL)	minced garlic
1 tsp (5 mL)	each chopped fresh thyme and oregano (or 1/4 tsp/1 mL dried)
1	jalapeño pepper, minced
12 cups (3 L)	mixed yellow and blue corn tortilla chips
8 oz (250 g)	Monterey Jack cheese, shredded

Fresh Salsa:

Mix tomatoes, onion, lime juice, jalapeño, coriander, parsley, thyme, oregano and green onion in a bowl. Refrigerate for 1 hour to blend flavours.

Refried Beans:

Mash beans with a fork or purée in a food processor. Heat oil in a skillet over medium heat. Add mashed beans, garlic, chili peppers and coriander. Cook for 3 minutes, stirring. Add salt to taste; reserve.

Guacamole:

Mash avocados in a bowl using a fork. Add lime juice, garlic, thyme, oregano and jalapeño. Stir well; reserve.

Place tortilla chips on a large ovenproof dish or platter. Distribute refried beans and salsa evenly over chips. Sprinkle with cheese. Bake in 400F (200C) oven for 5 minutes or until cheese is melted. Serve with guacamole on the side. Makes 6 to 8 small servings (double the recipe for larger appetites).

Pork and Beef Chili With Ancho Sauce

This is a very flavourful chili made with black beans, mixed meats and a shot of Prairie rye whisky. Serve it spicy-hot to chase away the chill, or make it milder and pass the chilies at the table so that people can add them to suit their own tastes.

2	dried ancho chilies
1/4 cup (50 mL)	olive oil
1 lb (500 g)	pork shoulder, cut into 1/2-inch (1 cm) cubes
1 lb (500 g)	beef chuck steak, cut into 1/2-inch (1 cm) cubes
1	large onion, chopped
5	cloves garlic, minced
1/4 lb (125 g)	hot Italian sausage, casings removed
1 tbsp (15 mL)	ground cumin

2–3 tsp (10–15 mL)	crushed dried chilies or hot pepper flakes (approx)
2	cans (19 oz/540 mL each) diced tomatoes
¼ cup (50 mL)	Canadian whisky
1 tbsp (15 mL)	dried oregano
1 ½ cups (375 mL)	cooked or canned black beans, drained and rinsed
¼ cup (50 mL)	tomato paste
	Salt and pepper

Soak ancho chilies in hot water for 20 minutes or until softened; drain. Chop, discarding stems and seeds; reserve.

Heat oil in a large Dutch oven set over medium-high heat. In several batches, cook pork and beef, turning often, until well browned. Remove with slotted spoon. Reduce heat to medium-low. Add onion, garlic and sausage. Cook, stirring to break up sausage, until onion is soft and sausage is no longer pink, about 4 minutes. Stir in anchos, cumin and crushed chilies and cook for 5 minutes. Stir in browned pork and beef, tomatoes with juice, whisky and oregano. Bring to a boil, reduce heat to low, cover and simmer for 1 1/2 hours.

Stir in beans and tomato paste. Simmer for 15 minutes longer to heat through. Add salt and pepper to taste. Makes 8 servings.

Coleslaw With Old-fashioned Boiled Dressing

Ranch cooks of yesteryear were never without boiled dressings, which they used to sauce up iceberg-lettuce salads and coleslaws like this one. This recipe makes extra dressing you can use as a dip or to dress another salad later in the week.

Dressing:

1 cup (250 mL)	granulated sugar
1/4 cup (50 mL)	flour
4 tsp (20 mL)	dry mustard
1 tsp (5 mL)	salt
1 cup (250 mL)	buttermilk
1	egg or 2 yolks, beaten
1 cup (250 mL)	cider vinegar
2 tbsp (30 mL)	butter

Salad:

1	small head green cabbage (about 2 pounds/1 kg), finely shredded
1	red apple (unpeeled), cored and grated
4	green onions, chopped
2	carrots, grated
	Salt and pepper

Dressing:

Mix sugar, flour, mustard and salt in a heavy saucepan. Whisk in buttermilk and egg until smooth. Slowly whisk in vinegar. Cook over medium-low heat, stirring constantly, until mixture comes to a boil and thickens. Reduce heat and simmer for 2 minutes. Add butter, stirring until melted. Pour into jar, cover and refrigerate. Makes 2 1/2 cups (625 mL).

Salad:

Combine cabbage, apple, green onions, carrots and enough dressing to moisten, about 1 1/4 cups (300 mL), in a large bowl. Toss well to combine. Season with salt and pepper to taste. Chill. Makes 6 to 8 servings.

Saskatoon-berry Potpie

This is a cobbler-like dessert with all the flavour of home-made pie but without the fuss of rolling out a crust. If you don't have Saskatoon berries, substitute blueberries; if using frozen berries, substitute cornstarch for flour.

6 cups (1.5 L)	fresh Saskatoon berries or blueberries
1/2–3/4 cup (125–175 mL)	granulated sugar
3–4 tbsp (45–50 mL)	all-purpose flour

Topping:

2 cups (500 mL)	all-purpose flour
2 tbsp (30 mL)	granulated sugar
1 tbsp (15 mL)	baking powder
1/4 tsp (1 mL)	salt
1/3 cup (75 mL)	shortening
3 tbsp (45 mL)	butter
1	egg
1/2 cup (125 mL)	milk
1 tbsp (15 mL)	granulated sugar for sprinkling on top

Toss berries with sugar and flour (if using blueberries, use the larger amounts of sugar and flour). Place in greased 8- to 10-cup (2 to 2.5 L) shallow oval casserole or other baking dish.

Topping:

Preheat oven to 425F (220C). Mix flour, sugar, baking powder and salt in a large bowl. With pastry blender, cut in shortening and butter until mixture resembles coarse crumbs. Lightly beat egg with milk and add to flour mixture, stirring and then kneading lightly to form a smooth dough.

Break off small chunks of dough, flatten to about 1/4 inch (5 mm) thick and place over filling to form a cobblestone effect, covering entire dish.

Sprinkle top with sugar. Bake in preheated oven for 35 to 40 minutes or until bubbly and topping is baked through and lightly browned. Makes 6 to 8 servings.

What to Serve With Ranch-Style Hospitality

This menu features comfort foods that will warm the heart as well as the stomach. Hearty wines will complement the hearty food in these recipes. A South African Pinotage will be a great way to start off this meal. The smoky and plummy flavours and aromas will complement the Black-bean Nachos. Thinking of the warmth of Africa while sipping this wine will help to drive away the winter chills.

The warm-climate wine theme will be continued with the wine selection to complement the chili. The chili has a big, robust flavour and is ideal for a California Zinfandel. The juicy mixed berry flavours in the wine will bring out the best in the dish. An alternative to Zinfandel would be an Australian Shiraz. These wines also show lots of ripe fruit and match well with foods with a little spice.

The dessert with Saskatoon berries is a natural to go with a Ruby Port. The warm fruit flavours will complement the dessert and leave a warm glow. If it is a special celebration, open up a Vintage Port, if not, a Late Bottled Vintage or a regular Ruby will work well.

Contributors

Wine Recommendations:
Suggested pairings are by Michael Fagan, Manager, Knowledge Resource Group, Liquor Control Board of Ontario. As the "Matchmaker," his product recommendations appear regularly in the LCBO's *Food & Drink* magazine.

Compiling Editor:
Dana McCauley,
Food Editor, *Homemaker's* magazine

Permissions Coordinator:
Amy Snider

Recipes by:
Julie Aldis

Karen Barnaby

Johanna Burkhard

Cinda Chavich

Carol Ferguson

Ruth Gangbar

Dana McCauley

Rose Murray

Anita Stewart

Food Photography by:
Michael Alberstat

Susan Ashukian

Clive Champion

Colin Erricson

Chris Freeland

Kevin Hewitt

Michael Kohn

Vince Noguchi

Michael Visser

Michael Waring

Copy editing and Index:
Mary Patton

Acknowledgements:
Without the many talented food writers and photographers who contribute to the pages of *Homemaker's* magazine, this book would not be possible. Thank you to all of you for sharing your talents so generously.

Index